The Handbook of Rugby

The Handbook of Rugby

Edited by Keith Miles

Contributors:

Dusty Hare

J. J. Williams

David Duckham

Les Cusworth

Nairn MacEwan

Peter Brown

Sandy Carmichael

PELHAM BOOKS

LONDON

PELHAM BOOKS

Published by the Penguin Group
27 Wrights Lane, London W8 5TZ
Viking Penguin Inc., 375 Hudson Street, New York, New York 10014, USA
Penguin Books Australia Ltd, Ringwood, Victoria, Australia
Penguin Books Canada Ltd, 10 Alcorn Avenue, Toronto, Ontario, Canada M4V 3B2
Penguin Books (NZ) Ltd, 182–190 Wairau Road, Auckland 10, New Zealand

Penguin Books Ltd, Registered Offices: Harmondsworth, Middlesex, England

First published in Great Britain 1995
Copyright © Keith Miles 1995

Typeset in Meridien Roman
Book interior by Design/Section
Printed and bound in Great Britain by
Butler & Tanner Ltd, Frome and London

A CIP catalogue record for this book is available from the British Library

ISBN 0 7207 1942 0

The moral right of the author has been asserted

This book is dedicated to rugby players everywhere – men, women and children. No disrespect is intended to the gentler sex by the use of 'he' and 'him' throughout the text. Everything is applicable to women as well as to men. No distinction is made between them.

Contents

Introduction

Rugby is the greatest of all team games and it has produced a rich and varied literature. This book is an addition to that sporting library, a comprehensive and authoritative manual that tells it like it is. It does not try to glamorise rugby or to conceal its inherent dangers. What it does set out to convey is the scope and the sheer excitement of the handling code. It is at once an instructional guide and a celebration of the game. Raw beginners will learn how to play from scratch. Battle-scarred veterans will be given a valuable refresher-course. Seasoned coaches will find their methods discussed or challenged. Referees have not been forgotten. Nor have spectators. *The Handbook of Rugby* has something to offer everyone connected with the game.

To fulfil these high ideals, a seven-a-side team of star contributors has been assembled. Collectively, they won over two hundred international caps between them and played the game with distinction in every corner of the globe. Their combined experience stretches back over three decades. But it was their individual qualities which gained them selection. Each man had a long and successful career on the playing field. Each has known the triumphs and perils of captaincy at club or international level. Each has shown a passionate interest in the development of the game. And each is a shrewd observer of the mysteries of rugby union. 'Learn from new books but old masters' advises a Turkish proverb. This new book offers you the combined wisdom of seven Old Masters.

Dusty Hare was an archetypal full-back whose presence on a rugby field could instil enormous confidence into the fourteen players in front of him. Rock-solid under the high ball and hard into the tackle, he was also a skilful attacker who knew how and when to come into the line. His career began with Newark in 1970 and ended at Twickenham almost twenty years later when this most durable of competitors was playing for Leicester in yet another Cup Final. He toured New Zealand with the British Lions, won twenty-five caps for England and made frequent appearances as a Barbarian. His record-breaking tally of over 7,000 points in first class rugby speaks for itself. For services to the game, he was awarded an MBE. Dusty Hare is the ideal teacher from whom to learn about all aspects of full-back play.

J. J. Williams was a classic winger whose thirty caps for his country coincided with the Golden Age of Welsh Rugby. He went on two Lions tours, scoring twelve tries for the 1974 team in South Africa. An international sprinter with an agile rugby brain, he was a supreme asset to any side and his mastery of the controlled chip over the heads of defenders will remain a vivid memory. In 1972 he moved from Bridgend to Llanelli and profited from the inspired coaching of the legendary Carwyn James. He scored 159 tries for the Scarlets and won all the club honours possible. His pace and flair were perfect for the Barbarian style of play. J. J.

Williams was a superb all-round winger whose emphasis on fitness was a key element in his game. In recent years, he has helped to improve the fitness training of the Welsh team and done an occasional stint as a television commentator.

David Duckham was also a world-class winger but it was as a brilliant centre that he first gained international recognition. He played for Coventry in its heyday and was a crucial figure in its cup-winning seasons. A big man with a blistering turn of speed, he had a swerve that could beat any defender. He toured with the 1971 British Lions, the only team to win a Test series in New Zealand. Converted to the wing position, he also shone in the epic Barbarian win over the All Blacks at Cardiff Arms Park in 1973. He won thirty-six caps for England at centre and wing, equally at home in either role. Nobody who saw him play for his country or for the Barbarians in concert with John Spencer will ever forget this most formidable of midfield duos. It is not surprising that David Duckham has such a keen eye for the finer points of centre play. He, too, was awarded an MBE for his services to rugby.

Les Cusworth was a textbook outside-half, a wily and effervescent player with an instinct for taking the right option in any situation. His first class career began in his native Yorkshire with Wakefield. He then played for Moseley before moving to Leicester. Like Dusty Hare, he drew immense benefit from the coaching of Chalkie White and went on to be a vital factor in the vintage years enjoyed by the Tigers. He was club captain in his final season of 1989–90. Twelve caps for England were buttressed by countless appearances in the colours of the Barbarians, Yorkshire, North Midlands, the Midlands Division and the Irish Wolfhounds. A supreme Sevens player, he coached the England team to victory over Australia in the final of the Rugby World Cup Sevens in 1993. He was also a drop-goal specialist and held the world record in the 1974–75 season when he dropped twenty-five goals for Wakefield. Les Cusworth was a thinking player with a touch of creative genius, an expert on the intricacies of half-back lore. He proved time and again that the smallest man on the field can often make the biggest contribution. As assistant coach to the England team, he continues to inject flair and expertise into the game.

Nairn MacEwan was a marauding flanker who wore the Scottish jersey in twenty-one internationals. His club rugby was played with Edinburgh Wanderers, Highland RFC, Inverness, and Gala. He also made almost fifty appearances for the North and Midlands XV and nine for the South of Scotland. He toured Japan and the Far East with the national side and South Africa with the Penguin International Select XV. His rugged commitment earned him a place in the Baa-Baas. Nairn MacEwan also has an impressive coaching record, including three years in charge of the Scottish team. He has been director of coaching with clubs in Italy, Sweden and Ireland as well as his native country. His book, *Basics of Rugby*, was published in Italy. Still deeply involved with the game, he is a true connoisseur of back-row play.

Peter Brown of Gala and the Barbarians won twenty-seven caps for Scotland and captained the side in some famous wins over the Ould Enemy. A prodigious lineout jumper, he could play in the second-row or at number 8 with equal facility. He was also one of the dying breed of goal-kicking forwards. His casual style might not delight the purists but it was remarkably effective at club and international level. Like his younger brother, Gordon, he was a dynamo in any pack. Peter Brown is still bound up with rugby and helps to organise the Bermuda Festival of Golden Oldies every year. If he kicked a ball from his house, it would land on the pitch of the adjacent Melrose RFC. From the same spot – at his peak –

he would have put it between the posts at Murrayfield. He combines a profound knowledge of the secrets of the second-row with a wonderful enthusiasm for the game.

Sandy Carmichael was one of the mainstays of the Scottish pack on fifty occasions, a powerful prop who gave no quarter. He played club rugby for West of Scotland and won every representative honour in the game, including a place on tours to New Zealand and South Africa with the British Lions. Former colleagues speak of him as a tower of strength and a fearless scrummager. Like David Duckham, he was a member of the revered Barbarians team which beat the All Blacks at Cardiff Arms Park in 1973. Sandy Carmichael has trenchant views on every facet of the game but his abiding interest remains the front-row. He still takes on coaching duties with senior players in Scotland and is also involved with a company which organises travel for rugby fans.

These seven respected voices talk with authority about their specialist areas.

They have not only been responsible for the sections of this book which bear their names. Their experience at the top level and their lasting affection for the game inform every page. Above all, they have stressed that rugby is to be played for enjoyment. Work hard, master the basics, refine your skills, set yourself higher targets all the time.

But never lose sight of the fun.

Dozens of other players and coaches have contributed indirectly to this volume and it would be impossible to list them all. I would, however, like to thank Terry Cobner, Mike Gibson, Fergus Slattery, Tony Neary and Ian McLauchlan for their advice in the early stages. My deepest gratitude once again must go to Roger Houghton of Pelham Books for giving me the opportunity to write about a game that I have played, coached and watched for almost forty years.

Keith Miles
May 1995

Key to Diagrams

Attacking player	○
Defending player	□
Line of running	⟶
Path of Ball	⇢

Positions in Rugby Union

1 Loose-head prop

2 Hooker

3 Tight-head prop

4 Second-row

5 Second-row

6 Blind-side wing-forward (or flanker)

7 Open-side wing-forward (or flanker)

8 Number 8

9 Scrum-half

10 Outside-half (or Fly-half or Stand-off)

11 Left-wing

12 Left-centre

13 Right-centre

14 Right-wing

15 Full-back

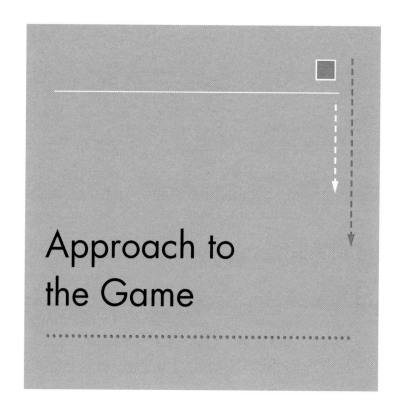

Approach to
the Game

The History of Rugby Union

Rugby has had a long and tempestuous history. Its precise origins are unknown but one thing is certain. It was not invented by William Webb Ellis when he violated the rules of football at Rugby School in 1823. The basic elements of the game had been in existence for several centuries before this time. To suggest that rugby union was born accidentally on a school playing field in Warwickshire is to ignore historical fact. William Webb Ellis belongs in the realm of myth.

Ball games go back to the dawn of civilisation. They were played for amusement and as a ritualised substitute for war between communities. The two sides battled fiercely for possession of the ball. Such contests often formed part of pagan religious festivals. Most of these games were more akin to rugby than to football for the simple reason that the ball was made out of stone, metal or wood and it was therefore too hard to kick. A handling code thus became essential.

Roman legions who occupied Britain in the fourth century used a game called *harpastum* as part of their training programme. It was played with a small round ball which was passed from hand to hand between players. Their objective was to cross the opposing line by use of force or guile. The Roman obsession with regimentation meant that the playing area was a standard rectangle with marked base and centre-lines. Players took up fixed positions and used a number of tactical ploys – like selling a dummy – which are still a feature of modern rugby. Tackling was an important aspect of *harpastum*. A very similar game, known as camp ball, survived until the nineteenth century in the eastern counties. It is surely no coincidence that a strong Roman presence was at one time centred upon Lincoln, Colchester and St Albans.

In his *Survey of Cornwall* (1602), Richard Carew writes of the traditional local game of *hurling*, which had a close resemblance to camp ball. It was of great antiquity and it was played with unrepentant ferocity. As Carew notes:

The play is verilie both rough and rude . . . When the hurling is ended you shall see them returning home as from a pitched battle with bloody pates, bones broken and out of joint and such bruises as serve to shorten their days.

A nation as boisterous as the Welsh did not miss out on the fun. On high days and holidays, they played a game known as *cnapan* which was little short of open warfare. By the time that George Owen of Pembrokeshire gave us the first recorded account of this turbulent pastime in 1603, it was already centuries old. *Cnapan* was a handling game that was played with a small, round, wooden ball that the bare-footed participants would not have dared to kick. The niceties of football were in any case out of the question because as many as two thousand people might be involved in a match. It was a cross country free-for-all that could lead to serious injury and even death. In a passage which foreshadows the team talks given to today's Welsh internationals before a match, George Owen

commented on the spirit of the game:

They contend not for any wager or valuable thing, but for glory and renown – first for the fame of their country in general, next every particular to win praise for his activity and prowess, which two considerations ardently inflameth the minds of youthful people to strive to the death for glory and fame . . .

Games like camp ball, hurling and *Cnapan* went into gradual decline as society in general became less combative and the open land where the sport had flourished was progressively enclosed. Play was sometimes translated to beaches or to streets in towns, with an inflated bladder supplanting the old wooden ball. Street football in Neath lasted until 1884. Cnapan had a final outing in 1922 at a game between Llandysul and Llanwenog. Societies which had been nurtured on such handling games adapted readily to the more controlled version known as rugby union.

Regional variations of football existed throughout the country from mediaeval times. Each shared common factors. The games involved enormous numbers. The ball was carried. The field of play was vast. Extreme violence was used to gain possession. Rivers, trees, fences, buildings or boundary marks were used to designate goal areas. Casualties were high. It is little wonder that the authorities dreaded the approach of holidays when the games were played. Shrove Tuesday was a particular cause for concern. The annual match held at Derby was so bloody and remorseless that its spirit lives on in the expression 'local Derby'. In the capital city, as elsewhere, an unruly populace could turn a football fixture into a riot that endangered life and destroyed property.

Philip Stubbes wrote in *Anatomy of Abuses* (1583):

> *football playing . . . may rather be called a friendly kind of fight than a play for recreation, a bloody and murthering practice than a felowly sport or pastime. For dooth not evryone lye in waight for his adversarie seeking to overthrow him and to picke him on his nose, though it be uppon hard stones . . . ?*

These communal exercises in uninhibited rugby were not confined to Britain. Like their Roman forbears, however, the Italians came up with a more organised and sophisticated version. In sixteenth-century Florence, games of *calcio* took place each spring. Each team had twenty-seven players. They lined up as three full-backs, four three-quarters, five half-backs and fifteen forwards. *Calcio* was played on a piazza roughly the size of a modern rugby field. The ball was carried,

passed and fought over. Matches lasted fifty minutes and were attended by enthusiastic spectators. A contemporaneous painting of a game held in Florence shows the forwards engaged in a maul while their respective back divisions wait for possession. Traditionalists have kept *calcio* alive in its native city in the twentieth century.

William Webb Ellis thus came very late on the scene. The rudiments of the handling code were already embedded in the national consciousness. At the point when he joined Rugby School as a day-boy, all the leading schools in England were playing a form of football that was

Reverend William Webb Ellis MA

dictated by the facilities available. Rules were continually changed in these other institutions as players sought to mould the game to their individual tastes and talents. What sets Rugby School apart from its colleagues is that the evolution of these rules was recorded. As a consequence, the improvised action of William Webb Ellis has taken on great significance and is immortalised in the famous plaque at the school:

THIS STONE
COMMEMORATES THE EXPLOIT OF
WILLIAM WEBB ELLIS
WHO WITH A FINE DISREGARD OF THE RULES OF
FOOTBALL AS PLAYED IN HIS TIME FIRST TOOK
THE BALL IN HIS ARMS AND RAN WITH IT
THUS ORIGINATING THE DISTINCTIVE FEATURE OF
THE RUGBY GAME
AD 1823

There are, however, other distinctive features of the game and Thomas Hughes made note of them all when he was a pupil at Rugby School in the 1830s. *Tom Brown's Schooldays* was written in 1857 by this other illustrious Old Boy. It evokes the Rugby of his youth and his veneration for its reforming headmaster, Dr Thomas Arnold. In the detailed account which Hughes gives of a game in his novel, we find the rugby field, the posts with a crossbar and the panelled leather ball that is oval in shape. Lineout and scrummage

are there along with the touchdown and the try at goal. These aspects of the game were evidently in place when Ellis was at the school in the 1820s so his alleged adjustment of the rules could not have been as revolutionary as has been claimed. What he did do was to take part in a process that resulted in the game of football being known as rugby.

Arguments over the rules persisted until two quite separate codes were established in the mid-nineteenth century. The rules drawn up at Rugby School formalised the handling code while the Cambridge Rules acted as the basis of what became the Football Association. Rugby spread quickly among public schools and universities. Blackheath formed a club in 1858. Liverpool, Richmond and Sale followed suit. In 1863, Richmond and Blackheath played each other for the first time in what is the longest-surviving regular fixture. Oxford formed a club in 1869 and Cambridge three years later.

The need to control the rapidly expanding game led to the inaugural meeting of the Rugby Football Union at the Pall Mall Restaurant, London on 26 January 1871. Twenty clubs attended. Two months later, the first international was played between England and Scotland. It took place in Edinburgh between two sides of twenty players. Since there was no referee, the captains of both sides were the sole arbiters in any disputes. This still obtained even when the Rugby Football Union drew up its new Laws that same year.

With a firm blueprint, the game developed apace. The Scottish Football Union was formed in 1873, the Irish Football Union in 1874 then the Irish Rugby Union in 1879. The Welsh Rugby Union came into being in 1880. International fixtures were arranged. The first Varsity Match between Oxford and Cambridge was played in 1872 and the Hospitals' Cup was founded in 1875. New clubs were sprouting up all the time. The game was also spreading overseas.

This period of growth was marked by some geographical variations. Rugby union rivalled association football in popularity among the working classes in Wales, in the West Country and in the North of England. But in Scotland and in the London area, the game was still largely the recreation of the public schoolboy or the university student. Its whiff of elitism was a serious obstacle to mass appeal. The ordinary working man liked to watch players rather than gentlemen.

The 1890s brought the game's greatest crisis. It arose from the concept of amateurism that lay at the very heart of rugby union. Love of the game was seen as an end in itself. It was to be played in a true Corinthian spirit without any thought of financial gain. By 1893, rugby union was being played throughout the British Isles by all classes. Time and money was being invested in the sport and the cost was a heavy one in some cases. This was especially true of clubs in the North of England where the bulk of the players came from the working classes and thus suffered a serious loss of earnings when taking part in matches or in tours. They sought compensation for 'broken time'. Representatives of clubs from Lancashire and Yorkshire were delegated to attend a general meeting of the RFU to press their case. Activists issued leaflets and circular letters to gather support against the proposed legislation. North and south divided irreconcilably.

The meeting was held at the Westminster Palace Hotel in London in an atmosphere of high tension. A record number of delegates heard the proposal of the motion, 'That players be allowed compensation for *bona fide* loss of time.' G. Rowland Hill, Honorary Secretary of the RFU and the most powerful figure in the rugby hierarchy, moved an amendment, 'That this meeting, believing that the above principle is contrary to the true interest of the game and its spirit, declines to sanction the same.' Amid acrimony, the amendment was carried by 146 votes, 120 of which were proxies gathered before the meeting even took place. Small wonder that the northern clubs felt hard done by.

Battle is joined: rugby in 1888.

The split between the two camps widened in 1895 when the Rugby Union tightened still further its legislation against professionalism. Twenty-two of the finest clubs in English rugby resigned from the RFU to form what they called a Northern Football Union. Rugby League was born, a thirteen-a-side game with no lineouts, rucks or mauls, and a play-the-ball rule after a tackle that made for almost continuous handling. Rugby football in England went into sharp decline. The number of clubs playing the game almost halved in the next ten years. The national side was so weakened that it did not win the International Championship again until 1910. The spectre of professionalism continued to haunt the RFU for the best part of a century. The commercial revolution within the game has made the issue even more pressing and divisive. Professionalism remains a stumbling block.

As England faded, Wales moved to the fore. Their finest hour was to come in 1905 against the mighty All Blacks. This touring side was nothing short of a sporting phenomenon. It arrived in Britain like a conquering army and cut down all who tried to stand in its way. Its impact on the public was shattering. No rugby team had ever combined such power with such technical excellence. Opponents were not just beaten. They were destroyed and forced to re-examine their whole approach to the game. When the tourists crossed the border into Wales, it seemed as if nothing could stop them from inflicting similar treatment on the national side.

The report in the *Daily Mail* on 18 December 1905, tells the story under the headline ALL BLACKS MEET THEIR WATERLOO.

The all-conquering 'All Blacks' have at last tasted the bitterness of defeat. After twenty-seven consecutive victories – nearly all of them of the most electrifying character – over the pick of English, Irish and Scottish rugby football, they were beaten by Wales at Cardiff on Saturday by one try to nothing amid a scene of indescribable Celtic excitement . . .

Wales went on to win seven Triple Crowns before the outbreak of war in 1914. It was not until England acquired Twickenham as their national ground in 1910 that their own fortunes began to improve. Rugby union continued to spread. New Zealand, South Africa, Australia and Canada were the other leading rugby-playing countries. The French Rugby Union was formed in 1910 after British students had taken the game across the Channel. It was moving further afield when the Great War halted its progress. Now the world was embroiled in a match that had no rules at all.

When peace finally came in 1918, rugby made a surprising recovery. Thousands of players had been killed in action but new ones took their place. Veterans returning from the wars tried to pick up their sporting careers. This was reflected most clearly in 1921 when the England pack which beat Wales had an average age of over thirty. It was during this period that the modern game evolved. British teams gradually adopted specialised positional play among their forwards. The South Africans patented the 3-4-1 scrum and the All Blacks were compelled to change their traditional use of only two men in the front-row. There were improvements in back play as well as a greater appreciation of tactics.

Features of the inter-war years were the rise of the French as a force in world rugby, the growth of Sevens, the influence of varsity rugby, the winning of Triple Crowns and Grand Slams, and the continued dominance of New Zealand. When the All Blacks returned to Britain in 1924, their superiority in technique, fitness and all-round teamwork was so great that they won all of their twenty-eight matches in style and scored over

650 points. In the same year, the British Lions struggled on their tour of South Africa. Although standards were rising all the time in the UK, they still fell short of what was being achieved by the All Blacks and the Springboks.

The Second World War ended countless rugby careers and truncated many more. Six long and oppressive years at once restricted and enlarged the scope of rugby union. While the game suffered on the home front, British soldiers exported it to countries in all theatres of war. Service internationals were staged to boost the morale of the civilian population and the temporary truce between rugby union and rugby league meant that spectators could see the giants of each code playing together on the same pitch. When the game eventually emerged from the war, it was in remarkably good condition.

A new dawn came. In an age of austerity, rugby enjoyed a boom and competed favourably in some areas with top football teams. At Cardiff Arms Park in 1951, for example, a world-record crowd for a club match of 48,500 saw the home team take on their arch rivals from Newport. The same venue was to reverberate even louder in 1953 when both Cardiff and Wales beat the New Zealand tourists. Of the countries in the five-nations championship, however, it was England who prospered most in the 1950s. During the next decade, it was Wales and France who led the way. Television had now arrived and was carrying the game to a much wider audience.

At the grass roots level, there were major developments. Schools taught the game eagerly. Representative games were arranged for more and more different age groups. Old Boys' rugby blossomed. The growth of higher education brought even more players into the common pool of talent. The first two decades after the war also witnessed the explosion of the worldwide game as new and more distant countries embraced its magic. Coaching was raised to new levels of excellence. The principle of squad training was accepted. Rugby League was still a potent threat, luring a steady stream of players to abandon the amateur code, but rugby union was nevertheless in good condition.

Politics threw dark shadows across the grass. The issue of apartheid came to a head during the 1969–70 visit to Britain by the South Africans. When protestors failed to halt the tour, they did their best to disrupt it and this partly accounts for the disappointing playing record of the tourists. The steady isolation of South Africa by world opinion meant that their rugby team was unable to play in Britain, Ireland, France or Australia after 1974. An ill-advised visit to New Zealand in

1981 was marred by bitter controversy and mass demonstrations.

British rugby had the best possible start to the new decade when the 1971 Lions became the first tourists ever to win a Test series in New Zealand. The coaching of Carwyn James on that tour was seen as a major factor in its success but he had a team of the highest calibre at his disposal. The British Lions sent an equally talented squad to South Africa in 1974 where they survived undefeated. Wales was in the ascendant in the five-nations championship with France providing immense flair and spectacle. England were rarely at their best and severely handicapped by the whims of their selectors. It was not until 1980 that they reasserted themselves to win the Grand Slam.

The 1980s brought major changes to the game both in structure and in the way it was played. Sponsorship rocketed as the Courage Leagues swept away the old system of friendly matches. The Pilkington Cup was the ultimate prize for the English clubs. Their Welsh counterparts fought for the Schweppes Challenge Cup, though it took a number of years before the benefits of a league system and merit tables were accepted in the Principality. As more money poured into the game at the top level, the distinctions between amateur and professional became a little blurred. Rugby union went on to make a dramatic

advance in 1987 when the first World Cup was held in Australia and New Zealand. Sixteen teams competed for the William Webb Ellis trophy. Predictably, it was won by the All Blacks who beat France in the final.

When the next World Cup was held in 1991 in Britain and France, the sport was given another superb shop window in which to display its qualities. England played brilliantly to secure a place in the final but it was the Australians who won the trophy. Earlier in 1991 the first Women's Rugby World Cup was held in South Wales. Teams from England, New Zealand, Canada, Wales, USA, Japan, Sweden, Spain, Italy, USSR and the Netherlands impressed everyone with the high standard of their play and showed what enormous strides forward the women's game had made. England reached the final but were beaten by the superior power of the USA.

As it is poised to move into the next century, rugby union is in good shape. Structure and organisation have improved greatly. Rule changes have, for the most part, made the game more attractive to play and watch. It may have vanished from the sporting curriculum of many schools as part of the pernicious philosophy that team games are in some obscure way harmful, but many clubs have started their own junior teams to introduce rugby to keen youngsters. The

World Cup Final: England v Australia, 1991.

bedrock of the game is sound and solid. If the huge amounts of money coming into rugby union at the top level are used wisely, then the long-term future is very secure. When the pupils of Rugby School played their matches, they were members of a highly privileged minority. The game has been completely democratised since then and exploded on a global scale. If the issue of professionalism can be resolved, the sport will continue to push out its frontiers.

Rules and Objectives

Rugby Union is played on a rectangular field with a maximum width of 69 metres and a maximum length of 100 metres. The dimensions of a rugby pitch should be as near as possible to these figures though most schools pitches – for obvious reasons – will be smaller.

The object of the game is to score more points than the opposing team by carrying, passing or kicking the ball. The team which scores more points wins the match.

The Pitch

The pitch is bounded by touchlines along each side and by goal-lines at each end. The lines are not part of the field of play. At each end of the pitch is an in-goal area, which extends a maximum of twenty-two metres from the goal-line. The goal-line forms part of the in-goal area but the dead-ball line, which termi-nates the in-goal area, does not.

Field of play and in-goal area together make up the playing area. It must be covered with grass or made of clay or sand. Whatever the surface, it must be level and free from any hard objects. Rugby pitches must be maintained in good condition.

Pitch Markings

A halfway line is drawn across the width of the pitch at a point halfway between the two goal-lines.

Another line is drawn across the pitch at a distance of 22 metres from each goal-line. This is called the 22-metre line.

Broken lines are drawn across the pitch parallel to the halfway line and 10 metres either side of it. These lines are known as the 10-metre lines.

A broken line is marked on the pitch 5 metres from each touchline and parallel to it. These extend the length of the pitch.

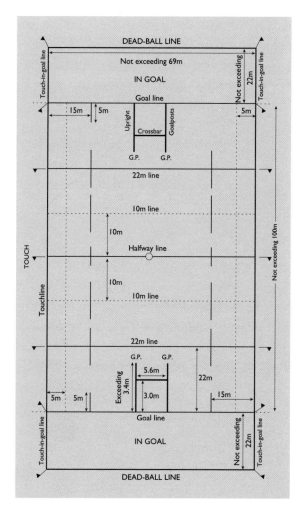

end of the two dead-ball lines to mark the outer limits of the playing enclosure. Additional flags are positioned at a point outside the touchline on each side of the field and adjacent to the halfway line and the 22-metre lines.

Fourteen flags are required. The recommended height of the flag-sticks is 1.2 metres. Flag-sticks should be made of bamboo or some pliable synthetic material that bends on impact so that players are not injured when they collide with them.

Goalposts

Goalposts are usually made of wood in an 'H' formation. The height of the uprights varies but there is a stipulated minimum of 3.4 metres. Most posts tend to be between 7.5 and 9 metres.

The distance between the two uprights is 5.6 metres and the

They do not go into the in-goal area.

Short lines intersect the halfway line, the 10-metre lines and the 22-metre lines at a point 15 metres from the touchline.

Flags

Flags are positioned at key points around the playing area. They are essential at each of the four corners of the field of play. They should also be placed at each

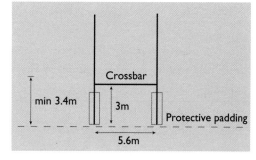

bottom of the posts should be padded to prevent injury as a result of collision.

The uprights are joined by a crossbar which is 3 metres above the ground. This measurement is taken from the ground to the top edge of the crossbar. The crossbar must not extend beyond the width of the posts.

Goalposts are erected at either end of the playing field in the middle of the goal-line.

Teams

A rugby team consists of fifteen players.

Forwards	
Prop	1
Hooker	2
Prop	3
Second-row/Lock-forward	4
Second-row/Lock-forward	5
Flanker/Wing-forward	6
Flanker/Wing-forward	7
Number 8	8

Backs	
Scrum-half	9
Outside-half	10
Left-wing	11
Left-centre	12
Right-centre	13
Right-wing	14
Full-back	15

Every match will thus involve thirty players. The only other person allowed on the field of play during a match is the referee. He will be supported by two linesmen who patrol their respective touchlines with a flag.

Numbering is now fairly standardised. Each number on the back of a player's jersey indicates his playing position.

A Match

Play starts with a toss of a coin between the two captains. The captain who wins the toss can choose either to kick off or to defend a particular end in the first half.

A match lasts for eighty minutes divided into two equal halves of forty minutes. Junior matches may be of shorter duration if agreed by both sides. An interval of up to five minutes is allowed at half-time. Teams must change ends for the second half.

Scoring

The object of the game is to secure possession, to gain territorial advantage as a result and to score points.

There are four methods of scoring:

1. **Try**	5 points
2. **Goal after try**	2 points
3. **Penalty goal**	3 points
4. **Dropped goal**	3 points

A try is scored by grounding the ball in the opposing in-goal area. The player must be holding the ball when he brings it into contact with the ground. He may also score if he falls on the ball with the front of the body and makes contact somewhere between his waist and neck.

A penalty try – also worth five points – may be awarded by the referee if he feels that a player was prevented from scoring a try by a deliberate infringement of the laws.

Every try is followed by a kick at goal. This is an attempt to convert five points into seven. The kick is taken at a point on the playing area directly in line with the spot at which the try was scored. It can either be a place kick or a drop kick. The ball must go over the crossbar and between the uprights. Both linesmen are stationed behind the posts to decide if the conversion has been successful.

Penalty kicks are awarded when the defending side commits an infringement. If the posts are within range, the kicker from the attacking team may attempt to score three points with a place kick or a drop kick. The ball must go over the crossbar and between the uprights.

Dropped goals can be scored by any player during open play. The ball must go over the crossbar and between the uprights.

Equipment

The Ball

The rugby ball is oval. It consists of four panels stitched together. The case was originally made of leather but synthetic materials are used today so that the ball does not absorb water in wet conditions.

Standard dimensions:
Length: ....280–300 mm
Circumference:
  (length-wise)......780–790 mm
Circumference:
  (width-wise).......580–620 mm
Weight: ....400–440 g.

Shirts, shorts, socks

All fifteen players should wear an identical strip. Shirts are normally numbered 1–15. They should be washed after each game and kept in a good state of repair.

Shorts should be a uniform colour and

The standard rugby ball.

made of a hard-wearing material. Socks will carry the club colours. They can be kept up with elastic garters or with tie-ups.

A rugby team should take a pride in its appearance. Players in ill-fitting jerseys or with shorts and socks that vary from the norm create a bad impression.

No player may take the field wearing dangerous projections such as rings, buckles or watches. Shoulder pads of the harness type are forbidden. If a player requires protection following a shoulder injury, the referee may allow the use of a pad of cottonwool, sponge rubber or other soft material.

Protective skull-caps are allowed. Players may prefer to protect their ears by taping them down or by wearing a headband. Crepe bandages and high-compression elastic supports may be worn.

Boots

These are a vital part of any player's equipment and must be selected with care. Some boots are built up to protect the ankle but the majority of players in the modern game prefer the low-cut boot similar to those worn by soccer players.

It is important to buy boots with two sets of studs, one long and one short. These can be screwed into the sole.

Longer studs will be used to provide grip on soft ground and the shorter studs will be needed for harder surfaces.

Studs must conform to the British Standard BS 6366: 1983. They must be circular, securely fastened to the boots and of the following dimensions:

Maximum length (measured from sole)	18 mm
Minimum diameter at base	13 mm
Minimum diameter at top	10 mm
Minimum diameter of washer (if separate from stud)	20 mm

The wearing of a single stud at the toe-end of a boot is prohibited. Before the teams take the field, the referee will inspect the soles of every boot to make sure that the studs conform to the legal requirements of the game.

Boot giving ankle protection

Low-cut boot

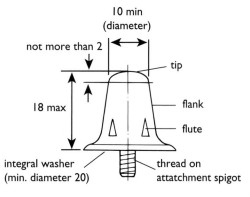

Studs must conform to the British Standard BS 6366: 1983. They must be circular and securely fastened to the boot. The wearing of a single stud at the toe of the boot is prohibited.

Officials

Every rugby match is controlled by three officials – a referee and two touch-judges or linesmen. It is important to understand their respective functions and to abide by their decisions during a match.

Referee

Only qualified referees should take charge of a game. They must be strictly impartial and apply the rules fairly and firmly. A good referee should be:

(i) Fit enough to keep up with play.
(ii) Conversant with the laws of the game.
(iii) Consistent in their application.
(iv) Clear and decisive.
(v) Able to remain cool under pressure.
(vi) Have a good positional sense.

A readiness to play the advantage rule is another asset and one that only

Penalty kick

comes with experience. It allows the game to flow instead of simply being a parade of stoppages.

International referees are of the highest standard but, even amongst them, interpretations of the rules can vary slightly. It is vital to obey the referee and to play to the whistle. A team must be able to adapt to each new referee and to play within his concept of the game.

Some judgements may be made about

a referee before he even takes the field. Good appearance and smart kit denote self-respect and a commitment to the sport. The referee's strip must be a complete contrast to those of the two sides so that he will stand out and not be mistaken as a player.

He will need a whistle to control the game and a watch to monitor its length. A spare whistle must also be carried and a second watch is a wise precaution. The other items needed are a pencil and pad. This enables the referee to keep a record of the score or to note down the name of any player whom he has to send off the field.

Certain signals are used to communicate a decision instantly to the players and to any spectators who may be watching.

Free kick

Try and penalty try

Touch-judges

The referee is the sole arbiter on the field of play and he is supported by the two touch-judges. At international level, they will themselves be qualified referees so that one of them can take charge of the game in the event of injury to the referee. All three officials in international matches

Advantage

Award of a scrummage

must be from neutral countries.

At club level, each team should supply a touch-judge to run the line. At half-time, the touch-judges will change sides. They will carry a flag and use it to attract the referee's attention. Their job is to advise when the ball or a player with the ball crosses the line and leaves the field of play. The flag will be raised and the other arm will indicate which side has the throw-in to the lineout.

The touch-judges must also help to adjudicate any penalty kicks at goal or any conversion attempts. They will station themselves behind the posts so that they are in the best position to decide if the ball goes over the bar and between the uprights. If the kick is successful, they will raise their flags. If it fails, they will hold their flags down and shake them.

In certain senior games, the touch-judges are empowered to report to the referee any foul play which may have escaped his notice. This is a vital role because even the most vigilant referee cannot police every incident that occurs in such a fast-moving game.

Like the referee, touch-judges must be fit, fair and decisive.

Watching the Game

One of the best ways to learn the game of rugby is to watch it being played properly. The higher the level, the greater the degree of skill and fitness on display. A World Cup offers a feast of rugby and an opportunity to assess the individual talents and techniques of the different countries. The five-nations championship is the annual tournament between England, Wales, Ireland, Scotland and France. Even the most partisan spectator can learn something from rugby of this quality.

If it is not possible to see these games live, try to watch them on television. What you lose in atmosphere you will gain in intimacy for the cameras are able to offer you insights into the game that are denied any spectator in a fixed position. But the best place to understand the game is on the touchline. Only there can you be part of the unique experience of a rugby match.

Senior club matches are played every Saturday afternoon during the season and there will be occasional evening matches midweek. Support your nearest club whenever you can.

It is difficult not to get carried away with the excitement of a game but the beginner should bear two things in mind:

1. Choose your Position

Use the game to help you select the position in which you should most enjoy playing and where your physique and skills would be best employed. Some positions are more glamorous than others but you must be realistic.

If you are very short and slight of build, then you are not a natural forward. If you are unusually tall and weigh over eighteen stone, you are unlikely to be a scintillating winger. Rugby can accommodate all shapes and sizes. Only by watching the game can you decide where you may find your ideal place.

Choosing between the forwards and the backs is the first step and sometimes taken for you by Nature. Selecting a particular position is more difficult. You may need to experiment with a few before you make your final selection.

Watch the game with special interest in the players on both sides who occupy the positions that appeal to you. See what their function is in the team and how well they discharge it. Though you will want to follow the ball, try to keep one eye on these players. Note what they are doing at every stage of the game.

A good role-model can be an inspiration to you.

2. Learn to Read the Game

However keen a supporter you may be of one team, respect the opposition and be ready to learn from them as well. Try to understand the tactics that are being employed by each side. Watch how one team will apply pressure to gain territorial advantage so that it is in a good position from which to strike for the line. Study the way in which the defending side absorbs that pressure and tries to relieve it.

Observe the scrummaging technique of both sides. Analyse the organisation of the lineout. Look at the alignment of the two back divisions. See where the full-back positions himself. Note how well-drilled a team is and how responsive to a captain's leadership. Recognise class play.

The more you study the game of rugby, the more you will learn. And the greater your insight into its mysteries, the more enjoyable it will be to watch and to play.

Do not forget the officials. Assess their contribution to the game. Weigh up all the factors involved so that each visit to a rugby match is not just an exhilarating event. It is a valuable learning experience.

Televised games also educate the spectator and instructional videos provide an excellent back-up. But rugby is played on a field of grass at the mercy of the elements. That is the only place to be on a Saturday afternoon during the season.

Fitness and Training

When rugby was a more leisurely game, some people played it in order to keep fit. That is no longer possible. Such are the demands of the modern game that you must get fit in order to play it. A high level of fitness has three cardinal virtues:

(i) You play the game better.
(ii) You enjoy it more.
(iii) You lessen the risk of injury.

Much of the work which is done at every training session contains a fitness element. Whenever you are running or involved in contact, you are strengthening muscles. All activity contributes to your general fitness but there must also be specific schedules to improve your fitness levels.

Sports science has now made inroads into rugby. Experts can evaluate individual performance and draw up schedules that are tailored to your own physiology. If problems are not entirely at the physical level, they can even draft in sports psychologists to improve your attitude to the game and to the preparation required by it.

The vast majority of clubs will not have such facilities. They have to include any fitness training in their normal sessions. Care must be taken to make this element varied and interesting. If you cannot afford equipment, improvise with the items which your club does possess.

Players must never be isolated. If suffering is a shared experience, it will be much easier to bear! In some areas, such as weight-lifting, assistance and supervision are vital. And all players perform better with encouragement from their team-mates. Pay full attention to the safety aspects.

Fitness Circuit

This can be used indoors or out of doors.
Set up a circuit that involves a repetition
of certain exercises. Fifteen to thirty
seconds should be spent on each exercise
before going on to the next. Movement
between the different exercises must be
continuous. Encouragement and moni-
toring from a coach or other players is
important.

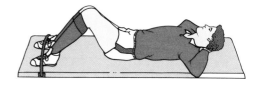

Sit-ups Lie on back with hands behind head and
knees up. Raise up into curl position and then
lower back down to floor. Build up speed.

A typical fitness circuit consists of:
Sit-ups
Star-jumps
Press-ups
Knees to chest
Vee sits
Squat thrusts
Back bends
Burpees
Legs raised
Bench jumps

Do not tackle similar exercises consecutively. Arrange the circuit to lend
variety and to take the strain off any
particular muscles.

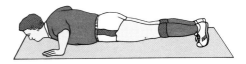

Press-ups Lie flat on chest with palms of hands
on floor. Raise body by using arms only. Hold
then lower. Repeat and build up speed.

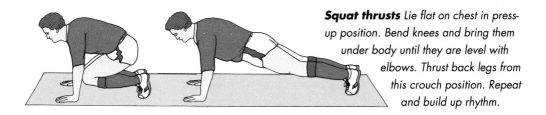

Squat thrusts Lie flat on chest in press-
up position. Bend knees and bring them
under body until they are level with
elbows. Thrust back legs from
this crouch position. Repeat
and build up rhythm.

Burpees *From a standing position, crouch on floor. Support body on hands and extend legs fully back. Bring legs forward into crouch position. Jump high with hands in the air. Resume crouch position.*

Bench jumps *Stand with legs astride gymnasium bench. Bring both feet up on to bench. Jump down. Repeat at speed.*

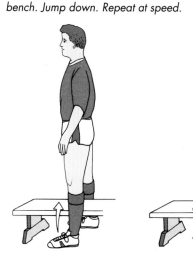

Skills Circuit

The skills circuit needs to be set up outdoors. Players must be made to work on the basic skills of the game in a confined area. A time limit adds incentive and speeds up the whole process. Running and passing exercises must operate in a grid, an area of the playing field that is divided up into squares. The size of the grid depends on the standard of the players. Raw beginners will work in much smaller areas.

A typical skills circuit should include:

Simple handling drill
Two-against-one drill
Support-play drill
Continuous-loop drill
Continuous-passing drill
Switch-pass drill
Scrum-half dive pass
Mauling
Jumping in the line
Scrummaging one-on-one
Fall and roll
Tackling
Shuttle runs

One-on one scrummaging

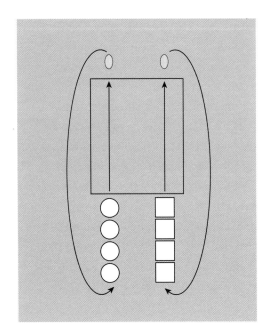

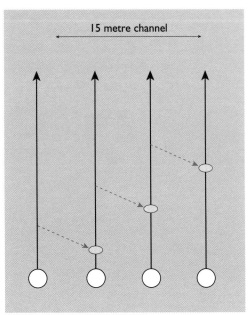

15 metre channel

(Top left) **Shuttle runs** Two or more teams in grid. First player runs to line with ball and puts it on ground. He runs back to team. Second player cannot move until touched. He reclaims the ball from line and brings it back to team, putting it on ground before third player, who takes it to line and leaves it there. And so on.

(Top right) **Continuous passing drill** At end of grid, turn to run and pass in opposite direction. Go back and forth. Reduce size of channel to shorten passes.

(Below) **Maul** Five against five. Ball kicked to defending side and caught. Maul develops. Ball released.

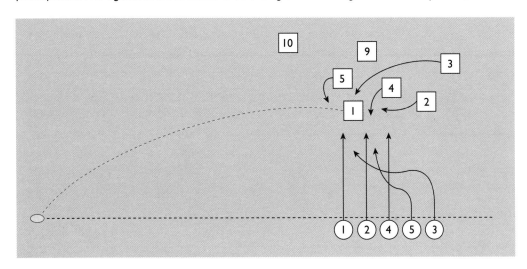

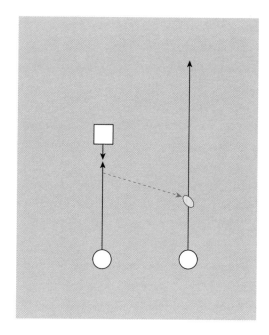

Two-to-one *Repeat exercise from side to side of the grid.*

The whole pitch may be used for sprinting practice. Diagonal runs from corner to corner of designated areas will test fitness and speed. Walking to the next starting point will give you a chance to recover. Increase the lengths of the sprint each time.

Agility runs can also be incorporated to make players vary their speeds and their lines of running. Cones are useful in marking out a training area.

Weight Training

Strength, power and muscular endurance are needed by all players. Weight training is a most effective way to build them up.

It must be supervised by a qualified coach. Never lift weights without someone in attendance. They can monitor your progress, give encouragement and move in quickly to assist if you get into trouble.

Each lift exercises a specific set of major muscles. A varied programme is needed to exercise the whole body.

Barbell

Power clean	Hips, legs, back
Front squat	Hips, legs
Bench press	Chest, triceps, shoulders
Arm curl	Biceps
Split squats	Quadriceps

Dumbell

Side bends	Abdominals
Jump squats	Quadriceps, hips
Crouching press	Triceps, shoulders

Machines can also be used to test particular muscles but some of these are highly expensive and beyond the reach of most clubs. If you cannot afford the basic equipment for weight training, improvise. A scaffolding pole set into two buckets of hardened cement makes a useful barbell. Dumbells can also be improvised. Make use of what is to hand.

Tailor weight training to the individual needs of players. Front-row forwards, for example, will require exceptional neck, shoulder and upper body strength. They must develop legs that can act as pit

Power clean

Front squat

props in a scrum. Back-row forwards need power and strength to push, maul, ruck and tackle but they must also work on flexibility. Each position has its special needs. Analyse them carefully and devise the appropriate weight-training schedule.

Training Sessions

Team practice must always be organised. The coach must know exactly what he wishes to achieve in each session with his team. Every player must be involved throughout. Give nobody a chance to become bored or disgruntled.

A fitness circuit and a skills circuit will occupy a small part of the session. Running practice is obligatory. But the coach will also want to work on unit skills and on team strategies. He may wish to iron out particular errors that have crept into the game or add new options to the attacking repertoire. It is up to him to make the training session a testing, productive and interesting event.

The coach must control the frequency and intensity of the training sessions. He must know how to bring his team to peak fitness and maintain that level. Under-trained players will flag during a game; over-trained players will suffer a progressive loss of performance. An experienced coach will know how much to train and how much to rest his players.

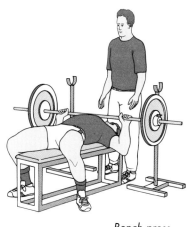

Bench press

Arm curls Split squat

Side bends

Crouching press

Jump squats

Training sessions must be hard but they must also be fun.

Mental Fitness

This is a vital component in the whole process. Physical fitness will never be demonstrated to its full potential unless a player has the right attitude towards the game. Mental preparation must therefore be taken very seriously.

Relaxation

Players must learn relaxation skills. Relaxation will not only promote rest and recovery, it will improve performance. It reduces anxiety and muscle tension. This is especially the case immediately before a game when some players may become so hyper-tense that they feel sick. It takes them time on the pitch to 'settle their nerves'. Learn to relax and to eliminate the collywobbles.

For deep relaxation, the simplest technique is to lie flat on the floor and reduce your breathing to a slower but still comfortable rate. Close your eyes and concentrate on one limb. Imagine that your left leg is getting progressively heavier as you relax the muscles. After a minute, repeat the process with your right leg. Then do the same with your right and left arms. Finally, concentrate on your trunk so that your whole body is now completely relaxed and free from any muscular tension. Sit up slowly, stretch then stand.

Concentration

Learn to focus your attention completely on the game in hand. You will only deliver a peak performance if your commitment is 100 per cent. Do not be distracted by spectators or by incidents that happen away from the ball. Block out all extraneous events. A full-back may be isolated for long periods from the ball but he must still follow its every movement and adjust his position accordingly. When you go on to a rugby pitch, leave everything else behind you. All your mental space must be occupied by the game.

Self-confidence

Many players have the ability to perform well but lack the confidence to prove it. Build your self-confidence all the time. It is a major component of your game. Monitor your performance so that you have visible evidence of your capability. If your standards are steadily improving, your confidence will be high. If there is a decline, analyse the reasons for it and address them with positive measures.

Watch those around you. It is both a learning experience and a source of confidence. Find role-models to imitate. Players of exceptional ability will always inspire confidence.

Good coaches will seek to boost the confidence of their players. Verbal persuasion from coaches or colleagues can help a player enormously. Do not seek false praise from others to boost your morale. Earn that praise by your performance on the field. Build on each success.

Team-work

Rugby is a team game and subject to group dynamics. It is also a contact sport and players rely on each other for physical protection. This will bond them closer together and promote a sense of team spirit.

Good team-work stems from an

understanding of others. Each player has a specific role to play on the field within a unit and within the overall performance of the team. It is vital for everyone to appreciate the contribution that his team-mates make in a game.

True cohesion takes time to develop. Scratch teams of famous internationals can often be beaten by club sides who play together every week and have better organisation and understanding. Familiarity breeds togetherness.

Team spirit must be developed off the pitch as well. This can be done in a number of ways:

Pre-game meetings – to prepare a team psychologically.

Post-game meetings – held at the next training session to analyse a game, to see what lessons can be learned from it and to set new team goals.

Team discussions – occasional meetings held to air a variety of topics in a relaxed and informal atmosphere.

Social events – these are not just a pleasant way of spending time with playing colleagues. They give the club a wider identity by bringing in its extended members and supporters and they help the team-members to relate to each other in the most easy and friendly way.

Mental fitness is not something which can be assumed. It must be worked on as systematically as physical fitness.

Injuries

Rugby is a high-speed contact sport and so there will always be a risk of injury. It can be minimised in two main ways:

(i) Technical know-how. Master the basics of the game and you will greatly reduce the chances of injury. Learn how to tackle properly and how to take a tackle; learn how to scrummage, ruck and maul; learn how to protect yourself in any contact situation that may arise in a game.

(ii) Fitness. Improve your speed, strength, endurance and flexibility all the time. This will enable you to avoid injuries that would be sustained by slower and weaker players. A high level of fitness is the best insurance policy against injury.

The front-row are in the most dangerous position and must take special precautions. Good binding, solid footing and timing of their shove is required. Collapsed scrums, violent wheeling and over-aggressive impact when forming the set scrum can lead to neck and back injuries. A front-row must be careful to avoid all three.

There are some other simple rules which will help to reduce the risk of injury on the field of play.

Protection

Gum shields protect the teeth and lessen the chance of more serious jaw injury and concussion. Forwards should protect their ears with tape. Front-row forwards may wear shin-pads.

Correct Kit

Jerseys and shorts should fit comfortably. An over-large jersey and baggy shorts can impede a player. Jerseys should be long-sleeved to prevent friction burns on the arms. Socks must be held up by garters or tie-ups to lend protection to the legs. Boots must be the right size and with the correct studs. Laces must be tied tight so that they do not trail and trip up a player.

Safe Environment

The pitch should be checked before each training session or match to make sure there are no sharp objects left on the grass. Heavy equipment or benches should be moved well back from the touchline so that there is no possibility of a player colliding with them if he is tackled into touch. The uprights of the posts should be padded and the touch flags must be easily knocked over on impact. If the training session or match is being held at night, ensure that there is adequate lighting.

If the training session is held in a gym, check that it is well-ventilated and well-lit. Make sure that there are no sharp edges around the perimeter. Doors and windows must be secured. Any equipment must be in good condition and safe for use. Equipment not in use must be stored away from the playing area or it may become a potential hazard.

Self-discipline

Do not be over-ambitious. Always play with and against people of your own physique and standard of play. Many injuries occur when forwards try to take on much stronger opposition; or when back divisions try to tackle much bigger and older opponents. Fair play reduces the risk of injury. A match between two well-balanced teams gives every player the best chance of looking after himself.

Warming-up

Always warm up before a match or a training session. In cold weather, wear a track suit as you go through your routine. Start slowly and gradually increase the intensity of your bending, stretching and jogging. When you take the field, you should be completely warmed up and ready for action. Repeat the process after the game or session. Cooling down is an important exercise. Gentle stretching exercises will help you to loosen your muscles and reduce the stiffness you may feel on the following day.

Hygiene

Regular showering or bathing is vital after any game or training session. Wash your kit regularly so that there is no danger of catching fungal infections of the skin. Do not borrow other people's clothing or towels as these may also carry infections.

Smoking and Drinking

Do not smoke. Cigarettes not only damage your health, they will impair your performance on the field. Nicotine affects the oxygen-carrying component of the red blood corpuscles and reduces the available space for oxygen to be supplied to the muscles. Never drink alcohol before a match or training session. It will affect your judgement and dehydrate the body thereby making it less efficient.

Diet

You need a balanced diet that gives you all your nutritional needs and provides energy. Allow at least two hours to elapse after a heavy meal before you play.

Planning

Plan your day so that you pace yourself. Most people need eight hours of sleep a night and time must also be set aside for training, eating, studying or working. Rest between training sessions and after games is essential or fatigue will set in. Inadequate rest is a major cause of most sports injuries and it weakens perform-ance on the field.

Plan your training schedule with care.

Overtraining will damage your health and your performance. Make sure that the coach does not give you too heavy a training-load. If fatigue does take over, rest completely for four or five days and increase consumption of fluids and carbohydrates.

Medical Problems

Take no chances. If you have a heavy cold or some other infection, do not train at all. Seek immediate treatment for any dental, skin or sinus problems as these can all hinder performance. Rest until any illness has passed. Every player should have a tetanus injection as a precaution with a booster when required.

Doping

Do not abuse drug-testing regulations, either by design or error. The Sports Council's Drugs Advisory Group will have an up-to-date list of banned substances. Avoid them all.

Rugby Injuries

Minor injuries – scratches and bruises – should be treated with First Aid. Every team should have an adequate First Aid kit on the touchline and someone quali-fied to use it.

More serious injuries like sprains,

strains, partial rupture of muscles or stress fractures of bones should be examined as soon as possible at the nearest hospital. Always err on the side of caution. Do not play again until you are fully recovered from the injury.

Fractures, dislocations and other serious injuries require immediate transfer to the nearest hospital. Make sure that the injured player is kept as warm and comfortable as possible while he is in transit.

Match Preparation

There is much more to this than simply learning the game and getting yourself fit enough to play it. A rugby match is a battle of wits and wills. A team must take the field with a game plan. Each player must know what his individual role is in the game and how best he can fulfil it. The coach will have drilled them and decided on the tactics to be pursued in a particular match.

Get plenty of sleep the night before a game. Avoid strenuous exercise the next morning. Eat a light meal a couple of hours before kick-off. Do not drink alcohol. Try to relax. When you reach the ground, the build-up for the game will begin. Concentrate solely on the job in hand. Listen to the coach and captain as they rehearse the tactical approach. Warm up in the changing room. Take the field confidently and have a short sprint to get your lungs working.

Play the game with controlled aggression that always stays within the bounds of the law. Do not be provoked by foul play on the part of your opponents. Self-discipline is the mark of a good player. Lose your temper and you let down the whole team as well as yourself. If you get sent off for violent behaviour, it is a slur on the reputation of your side. It will also weaken your chances of future selection.

Display the right attitude. This is enshrined in the Rules:

> *The Object of the Game is that two teams of fifteen players each, observing fair play according to the Laws and a sporting spirit . . .*

Rugby is all about sportsmanship. Determination and will to win must fuel any team but it must operate by fair means. Noisy, argumentative, ill-disciplined teams do the game no service at all. Brawls only disfigure a match. Players who feel aggrieved by their own colleagues should take the matter up with them in the changing-room after the match. Dignity and equanimity must be preserved on the pitch at all times.

Every team wants to win but it is important to do so with style. Good behaviour is its own best advertisement.

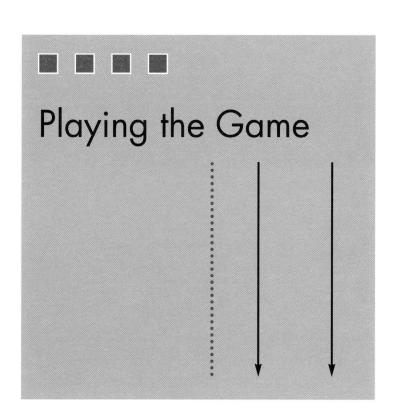

Playing the Game

Individual Skills

Running

Running rugby is the most attractive to play and to watch. But an expansive game is only possible if players develop and hone their running skills. It is not simply a case of learning to sprint. Speed alone is not enough. Balanced running is the order of the day. You must be able to change pace and direction at will and to ride the half-tackle. Many famous sprinters have been found wanting on the field of play. Supreme in the hundred-metre dash, they cannot adapt to the obstacle race that is rugby union – especially when the obstacles go on the attack!

Practise running with a ball. Tuck it in under one arm and close to your chest. Hold it securely so that it cannot be knocked away by the force of a tackle. Your other arm is free to aid running or to be used for a hand-off. You must always be able to get two hands on the ball instantly in order to be able to pass it.

Forwards will tend to make short surges in confined spaces before meeting opposition. Ball retention is especially vital here. Close passing must be mastered.

The back division will have more opportunity to create and exploit space. They must have confidence to take on and beat their man with elusive running.

The Side-step

The side-step is a sudden change of direction. It requires perfect timing but it will beat any defender. A player who can side-step off either foot is a danger. The secret is to disguise your intention to the last moment. When the defender closes in on you from an angle, come off one foot to alter your direction and go past him.

Practise on the training ground until you have mastered both the timing and the surprise element. You must also ensure that there is no loss of speed.

Pace, power, class *Andrew Harriman is the epitome of balanced running.*

Work in a grid with the other players.

Reverse the direction of the practice so that you come off your left foot. If the defender slows down to counter your side-step, you accelerate and beat him on the outside. Even in limited space, a side-step can be devastating and it may not only beat one defender. If the cover is streaming across the field, a double or even treble side-step is sometimes possible for the real expert.

Swerve

When the defender is not close enough

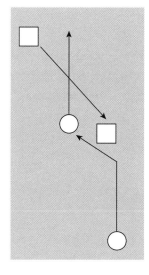

The Side-step
Attacker in centre of grid. Try line adds incentive. Defender in corner of grid. When side-step off right foot is perfected, switch defender to other corner. Attacker now has to side-step off left foot to beat his man and score.

(Left) *All Black John Kirwan demonstrates his devastating swerve.*
(Right) *Rory Underwood at speed, holding the ball correctly, ready to pass if necessary.*

to be beaten by the side-step, a swerve may be more effective. Run towards the defender, feint to go in-field to slow him, then swing your hips and accelerate away in an arc on the outside of him.

Practise in a grid, taking the ball at speed and trying to beat the defender on either side by wrong-footing him. You may also use a hand-off to assist the swerve. In the right circumstances, the combination of the two can be lethal.

Passing

This is a core skill of the handling code and it cannot be practised enough. Ball-handling must be at the heart of every training session. When you have possession and are about to give a lateral pass, hold the ball in front of you with your hands either side of it.

Look up to see where you are passing and make sure that the ball is thrown in front of the catcher so that he can run on to it. If you pass directly to him, he will have to check his run to take it. Forward passes are illegal so pass the ball behind you but in front of the catcher.

Before you pass, draw your man. Commit a defender and then release the ball. If you are passing to your left, the weight of your body is on your right foot

Roy Laidlaw of Scotland gets his back-line going with a perfect pass.

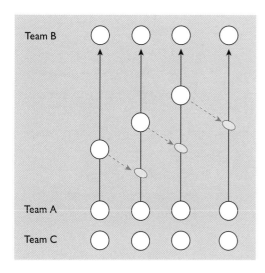

so that you can swivel your hips and face the catcher. If you pass to your right, the weight of your body will be on your left foot at the moment of release.

Passing exercise *Team A passes ball from left to right until they reach the line. They give the ball to team B, who pass the ball along the line until they reach the opposite line. Team C repeat the drill and hand over to Team A, who have re-formed on the line. And so on. Vary the lengths of the passes each time. Switch direction of passing. Then repeat continuous drill.*

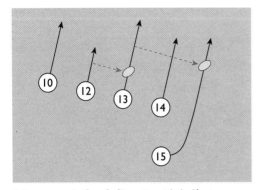

Miss pass in back line *Outside-half misses out left-centre and passes direct to right-centre. Right-centre misses out wing and passes to full-back, who is creating the overlap by coming into the line.*

Specialist passes from scrum-halves are discussed elsewhere but every member of the team must be able to vary the length of their passes. Practise in a grid and pass the ball along a line at speed. Double the gap between each player so that each must give a long, accurate pass. Reduce the gap so that crisp, close-passing is required. And so on.

The SCISSORS or the SWITCH PASS can be an effective way of changing the direction of attack or breaching a defence. It requires a good understanding between the passer and the catcher and must have the surprise element. The ball carrier runs slightly across the field and turns to show the ball to the receiver. The latter cuts in close at an angle so that he can take the ball and accelerate away.

The MISS PASS can be used to miss out a closely marked attacking player and to get the ball quickly to an unmarked colleague. It can also be used to speed up the transfer of the ball when an extra man joins the line. It relies on timing and accuracy and must be practised regularly.

Catching

Passing and catching go – literally – hand in hand. The dropped pass in a scoring opportunity is a major crime. Catching is not aided by the shape of the rugby ball. The golden rule is to keep your eye on the ball until it is safely in your hands. Let the ball come into your body and always use two hands to catch it.

Fielding the high kick is a vital skill, especially as it may be accompanied by

Scooping the ball off the ground.

rampaging attackers. Keep your eye on the ball again. Make a cradle of your arms so that the ball can fall into it and you can bring it to your chest.

Taking the bad pass is also an invaluable skill. There will be occasions when you have to scoop it off the ground or pluck it out of the air like a basketball player. Safe hands come from constant practice. If the ball goes to ground, try to pick it up in one continuous movement and carry on with the run.

Tackling

The bigger they are ... A textbook side tackle on Ben Clarke.

Tackling is an important part of the game and the correct techniques must be learned. Safety is a key element. If they tackle properly, players will not be hurt. It is vital for the tackler to keep his head behind or to one side of the oncoming attacker. The shoulder must be the first point of contact, followed by the arms which wrap around the legs.

Side Tackle

This is the most common tackle in the game because you will be coming in at an angle on the ball-carrier. Your target area is the line of shorts and thigh. Go in hard and low.

(i) Make shoulder contact with your opponent's thigh to knock his knees together.

(ii) Keep your head behind his buttocks.
(iii) Wrap your arms tightly around his thighs.
(iv) Hang on till he falls and land on top of him.

Raw beginners may need to practise without boots on so that accidental damage is avoided. Always let the player to be tackled have the ball and a try-line to aim at. This will give him incentive and add realism. Start with a slow run so that the tackler is hitting a moving target. As proficiency improves, the tackler must take out his man at top speed.

Front Tackle

Use the attacker's momentum to complete the tackle. Follow the same principles as

Prop v. full-back. Jeff Probyn about to execute a front tackle on Serge Blanco. Rear ventilation in Probyn's shorts is optional.

player matures because it needs expert timing and accuracy to avoid injury.

There are occasions when the standard front tackle will not suffice. If you are close to your try-line when you hit the attacker, his momentum will carry him over. It is thus vital to stop him in his tracks. This may be done with a crash tackle or a smother tackle, where you wrap your arms round his upper body and round the ball. If the attacker is too big and heavy to check, try to stay underneath him as he knocks you backwards over the line. You will then prevent the ball being touched down and save a try.

Tackle from Behind

This can be dangerous if your technique and timing are at fault. Try to get to your opponent before he builds up speed and has his heels kicking up fully behind him. Your target area once again is the line of shorts and thigh.

with the side tackle. Drive in low and hard at the line of shorts and thigh. Your shoulder makes the contact, your head is to the side. Wrap your arms around his legs and hold tight. Allow his momentum to complete the tackle by falling backwards. As you hit the ground, turn your opponent so that you finish on top.

Some players favour the crash tackle, coming in with such force from the front that they knock their opponents over backwards and sometimes dislodge the ball. A good crash-tackler will always be feared but this is not a tackle for the beginner. It is a skill to be developed as a

(i)   Go in low to make shoulder contact.
(ii) Keep head to one side of hips.
(iii) Wrap your arms around his thighs and pull tight until he falls.
(iv) Turn to the side on impact with the ground so that you finish up on top.

If the player has built up speed, it may be necessary to go into the tackle slightly higher. Hit your man around the waist and let your arms slip down to complete

Will Carling is stopped by Brendan Mullin's determined tackle from behind.

the tackle and topple him to the ground.

This tackle needs to be taught properly. Beginners may find it easier to use a tackle bag to build up confidence as they run in hard to effect the tackle. When they first practise with an opponent, the ball-carrier should remove his boots so there is no danger of serious injury to the tackler.

Smother Tackle

This is designed to prevent the ball-carrier from passing to a colleague. Go in hard and wrap your arms around his upper body so that he is unable to release the ball. The force of your tackle should knock him to the ground and you should finish up on top of him.

Tackling must not be seen solely as a chore. There must be an element of fun as well as a skill factor. A team of committed tacklers will always earn the respect of their opponents. Tackling should form part of training sessions but must not be overdone. Little and often is a more practical way to improve tackling. Recreate match situations on the practice field so that tackling has real purpose.

Kicking

Dusty Hare

Kicking is an important feature of every game. The full-back and the two half-backs will do most of the kicking but each member of the team should master the basic skills. Even a front-row forward may be called upon to kick to touch under pressure. And every player is able to make a mark after a fair catch behind his own 22-metre line.

The Punt

This is used to gain touch; as a high kick to be chased by the attacking side; as a long diagonal kick to gain ground; or as a cross kick.

Hold the ball at an angle pointing towards the touchline. The right foot should be used for kicks to the left-hand touchline. The left foot should be used for kicks to the right-hand touchline.

Keep your eye on the ball throughout. The left hand is placed to the side of the ball and the right hand is slightly on top. Fingers are spread wide.

Arms are held forward. The ball is placed along the kicking foot in the same direction that it is being held. Kick through the ball. Your body weight should move forward to give added power. Timing and balance are vital elements.

At the moment of impact, the kicking foot should be at roughly the same angle as the ball. The instep makes the contact. A good follow-through will give more distance.

This punting technique will produce the screw kick, with the ball rotating as it flies through the air. It needs a lot of practice to get length and accuracy. Even specialist kickers must work hard to polish their skills.

Practise with a partner. Both of you will then be rehearsing your catching skills as well as your kicking to touch.

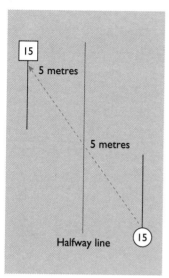

15

↖ 5 metres

5 metres

Halfway line (15)

Kicking practice
Full-back and partner stand some distance apart, five metres out on different sides of halfway line and kick to touch in turn.

Stand on the halfway line. The distance between you should be your maximum kicking range.

Both of you step five metres to the right. Kick the ball to each other, trying to get full distance on each punt so that it lands up only five metres over the touchline. Do not waste your power by putting too much height on the ball or by sending it deep into touch. Your partner is the target. He uses you in the same way.

Vary the practice by moving out another five metres to give yourself a better angle. Repeat the exchange of touch kicks. When you have developed your technique and accuracy, go back to the halfway line then move five metres to your left.

Exchange kicks with your left foot. The distance between the two of you may need to be shortened if both of you are now kicking with your weaker foot. Move out in time to widen the angle.

Practise also in adverse weather conditions so that you learn how to cope with a strong wind.

The High Kick

The up-and-under is an excellent way to turn the opposition and put them under pressure. The high punt must hang in the air so that the attacking side have time to race to the point of descent. The defender who catches the ball should be tackled simultaneously.

A practice routine for the high kick – and for defending against it – is given in my section on full-back play.

The Diagonal Punt

This kick is most often used by the outside-half who puts the ball diagonally over an advancing back division towards the far touchline. He may wish to gain ground by putting the ball into touch. Or his kick may be angled for his winger to run on to it and gather.

Other members of the back division should also be able to put in a well-judged diagonal kick in attacking or defensive situations. Regular practice of the diagonal punt with partners is important.

The Cross Kick

This is not a major feature of the modern game but it can still be very effective. The typical cross kick comes from a wing who is put past his own man but hemmed in by the cover. Instead of being caught in possession or bundled into touch, he can put in a cross kick to change the direction of attack. Supporting players coming up the middle of the field will be in a position to collect the ball or to tackle any defender who gets to it first.

The Chip Kick

This is a little punt over the heads of advancing players. The ball will be gathered either by the kicker himself or by a

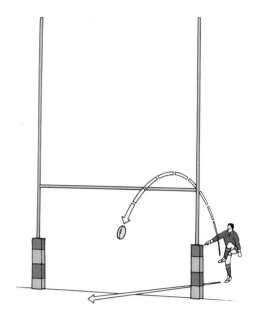

Chip kick *Kicker runs towards goalposts, chips the ball over crossbar and runs on to catch it. Repeat exercise in opposite direction. Go to and fro until the chip kick is perfected.*

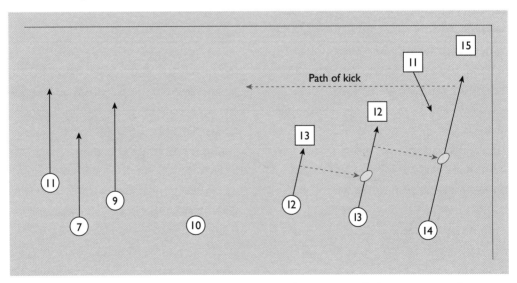

Cross Kick *Winger goes outside his man down touchline then uses cross-kick to supporting players in the midfield.*

team-mate who may be following up.

As with all kicks, timing is vital and this can only be developed by long practice. A solo exercise is for a kicker to chip the ball over the crossbar then run between the posts to catch it. But it is always best to work with partners on the training ground.

Grubber Kick

The grubber should be part of every kicker's repertoire. It can be used in attack when you want to put the ball behind an advancing defence. Or it is a way of putting the ball into touch when outside your own 22-metre area.

Hold the ball sideways with your left hand on top and right hand below. Drop the ball beside the non-kicking foot. As the ball touches the ground, the kicking foot swings through to make contact with the instep. Keep your eye on the ball and your head over it.

When you have mastered the grubber kick, the ball should travel along the ground like a torpedo. Regular practice with other players will enable you to increase length and accuracy.

The Drop Kick

Unlike the kicks so far discussed, the drop kick can earn three points. It is a potential match winner and deserves close attention.

Grant Fox: the drop kick that garnered such vital points for New Zealand.

The drop kick is used to restart the game from the 22-metre line or from the halfway line after a conversion attempt or penalty goal. When an attacking side is within range of the opposition posts, it is a valuable scoring option.

Hold the ball with both hands so that it is pointing towards the ground. As you take a step forward, drop the ball to land on its point opposite the non-kicking foot. Swing the kicking foot through to make contact with the ball as it touches the ground.

Angle your foot down so that impact

Drop kick *As the ball bounces, the player's foot catches it on the half-volley.*

is made with the instep. Use a high follow-through to lift the ball into the air. Eyes must stay on the ball and head must be over it.

Restarts should be practised with a full pack to follow up your drop kick. Use a partner to practise the dropped goal. Kick it to each other between the posts, varying your distance and angle each time. This exercise will also give you good catching practice.

The Place Kick

There was a time when goal-kickers used to place the ball upright and kick it low down with their toe. From longer distances, they sometimes used the torpedo kick, where the ball was angled forwards so that one of its points was facing the posts while the other end was struck with the toecap.

Great kickers, like the late Sam Doble, pioneered a technique which has completely taken over. This is the round-the-corner method that is used by most top kickers in the game and it is the one that I perfected in my own playing career.

Here are the checkpoints:

(1) Place the ball to tilt slightly forward.
(2) The lace – or the 'front' of the ball – should point towards the centre of the posts.
(3) Put your non-kicking foot beside the ball then step backwards the requi site number of paces.
(4) Run up until your non-kicking foot is again level with the ball then swing your kicking foot.
(5) Hit the ball low down and make a firm connection with your instep.
(6) Push-through the ball to get maximum power.
(7) Aim for the target you have set yourself.
(8) Eyes on the ball throughout.
(9) Head over the ball at the point of contact.

Concentration and timing are vital. They will only come from long and systematic practice. Do not try to overdo the power in the kick. Keep your engine running smoothly. A goal kick must be

Gavin Hastings: a study in balance, power and timing.

executed in one clean and fluent move.

From close range, I tended to chip the ball over, almost like hitting a wedge shot on a golf course. From further out, I took a longer run and had a fuller follow-through with my kicking foot. I worked on range and accuracy all the time.

At international level, specialist goal-kickers should have a high percentage of success within forty metres of the posts. Beyond that range, an element of doubt will creep in.

To succeed with a kick from outside your own half, you need a long run-up, firm contact with the ball, a complete follow-through and the right trajectory.

Goal kicks win games. Long hours on the practice ground can be turned into points in matches. Establish a routine for each kick and stick to it. This will help concentration. All the great goal-kickers have their own individual ritual. Find the one that suits you and pays the best dividends.

Do not forget to practise in adverse weather conditions as well. Put yourself under pressure. Learn to use a swirling wind or to combat driving rain. In bad conditions, which do not favour handling, games are often decided by the boot.

The laws now permit the use of sand and of plastic tees in which to place the ball before a penalty kick or conversion attempt. These are especially useful on very hard grounds. Experiment with all the possibilities. Settle on the one that gives you the most consistent results. And good luck!

Full-Back

Dusty Hare

In the old days, full-backs were seen simply as the last line of defence. They were lonely figures who stayed in isolated positions behind their back division. They only came into the game to field the ball, kick to touch, tackle or take a penalty.

Modern full-backs are very different. While they must still be rock-solid in defence, they are also key figures in attack. Full-backs like J. P. R. Williams of Wales and Andy Irvine of Scotland were great opportunists who knew when to join the back-line as an extra man in attack. They also had the confidence to launch counter-attacks from deep positions with the help of their respective wings.

Serge Blanco was another supreme example of the all-round full-back. His defence was sound and his running abilities were amazing. Like J.P.R. and Andy Irvine before him, he has scored many crucial tries at international and club level. These players are all models to copy.

The perfect full-back would combine the attacking skills and aggressive tackling of a J. P. R. Williams; the speed and flair of an Andy Irvine; and the goal-kicking accuracy and consistency of a Dusty Hare. Throw in the power and positional sense of a Gavin Hastings for good measure and you have a world-beater.

Defence

The defensive qualities of a full-back still come first. He must be:

(a) Safe under the high ball.
(b) Sound with his line-kicking.
(c) Secure in the tackle.

The high ball is a deliberate test of a full-back. He must have courage, coolness under pressure and technique. Watch the ball every inch of the way. Get into a position to catch it. Face the nearest touchline so that you can use a swift kick to put the ball out. Again, if you drop the ball in this position, you will not have knocked on.

Keep the feet well apart to give you a firm base. If you get ball and attackers at the same time, you will take the tackle sideways on. Turn your back into the oncoming attackers and try to stay on your feet as your own players give support.

If you are close to a touchline as tacklers converge, you may sometimes be able to drag them and the ball over it.

The most difficult situation for the full-back is the high ball which lands just in front of the posts. Both touchlines are a long way away and you can feel stranded. It is the acid test of a full-back. Regular practice of this situation will give you technique and confidence.

Here is a simple exercise for the training session. Put the full-back between the posts. Use another player to hoist a high kick that hangs in the air. This will probably be the outside-half

Winger Tony Underwood collects a kick with full-back Jonathan Callard in close support.

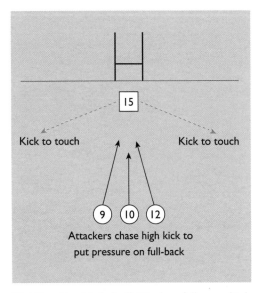

Kick to touch

Kick to touch

15

9 10 12

Attackers chase high kick to
put pressure on full-back

Fielding the high ball *Attackers follow up high kick to put full-back under pressure.*

because he is the most likely player to use this ploy against an opposition full-back in a game. He will thus be getting valuable practice along with his own full-back.

Each ball will come down in a slightly different way. The full-back has to catch the ball each time and kick to touch, alternating between the two touchlines. Ability to kick with either foot is a great asset. During a game, you may not always have time to put the ball on to your stronger foot.

When the ball is kicked to touch, there should always be a target area marked. This could be done with cones or with other players who would themselves be gaining valuable catching practice.

After kicking one ball to touch, the full-back runs back to touch a goalpost. That is the signal for the next high kick. Eye on the ball, he makes a firm catch and kicks to the other touchline.

Make it potentially more dangerous by having attackers put him under pressure as the ball comes down. This gives other players practice in sprinting after the high kick to harry the full-back.

Increase the number of attackers to apply maximum pressure. The full-back may still be able to catch and kick. If he takes the ball with both feet firmly on the ground, he may make a mark and then kick through it to touch.

Another option may be used if a defending wing is brought into the practice. The full-back will catch, run and pass to the wing who is better placed to kick to touch.

Positional play is essential for a full-back. He must be able to read the game so that he is in the right position to take the high ball. He may not always be static when he does so. Catching the ball on the move is a more difficult skill but one which must be mastered. It usually gives the full-back more options as a moving target is less easy to hit. If he can take a high ball at speed, he may be in a position to turn defence into attack.

The high ball may be a deliberate up-and-under or a kick to touch which remains in play. Equally problematical is

Gavin Hastings joins the attack to burst down the blind-side.

the rolling ball. This may come from a diagonal punt, a grubber kick or simply arise when an attacker hacks the ball through along the ground.

The full-back finds himself chasing the ball and running back towards his own goal line. This will always occur in a game and must be practised thoroughly.

Stand fifteen metres from the touchline on your own 22-metre line. Get another player to roll the ball hard towards your goal line. Chase, fall, collect the ball, get up and clear it. After several repetitions, this exercise can be transferred to the other side of the pitch to work the other touchline.

Once the full-back has perfected his

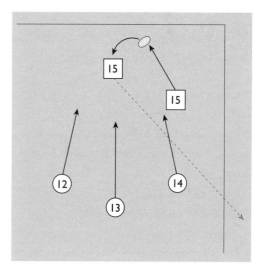

Chasing a rolling ball *Once the exercise is perfected in this corner of the field, transfer to the other corner so that the full-back has to use his left foot to kick to touch.*

technique, add pressure by sending an attacker after him. The running line of the attacker will determine which way the full-back turns and which foot he uses to kick.

If two attackers are used to harry him in this confined part of the pitch, he will have to improvise even more.

The full-back is not only honing his retrieving, handling and kicking skills. There is a strong fitness element in the exercise for him and for other players.

Line-Kicking

Every full-back must be adept at line-kicking in all weather conditions. A swirling wind may be used to advantage when it is at your back. If you kick into a strong wind, use a lower trajectory and settle for less distance than you would normally get. Safety is the watchword. Put it in touch.

If you are outside your own 22-metre line, your kick must bounce the ball into touch. This art can only be mastered with long practice. Use other players in this practice so that you learn how to kick instinctively into the spaces.

When you field the high ball, you may not always have to kick to touch. If you have time, it may be possible to chip over the advancing attackers and chase. You may even reply with an up-and-under of your own. It is vital to race after such a

kick at full speed to harry the defender who catches it and to put your own players back onside.

Tackling

Effective tackling depends on being in the right position. When the opposition launches an attack, the full-back is a crucial part of the defence system. He must know which system is being used and which attacker he is covering.

Man-for-Man Defence

Most defending sides use this system when the opposition have the put-in at a scrum in a good attacking position. Each player takes his opposite number.

If the attacking full-back comes into the line to make the extra man, he must be covered by the defending full-back.

An alternative here is for the defending wing (14) to take the full-back who intrudes into the line while his own full-back takes the job of tackling the attacking wing (11).

There must be good communication between defending backs. As they move up in line, they must know who will tackle whom.

The defending full-back must get up quickly on his man to apply pressure and cut down his thinking time. Keep on the inside of your target so that he is forced towards the touchline. If you have to

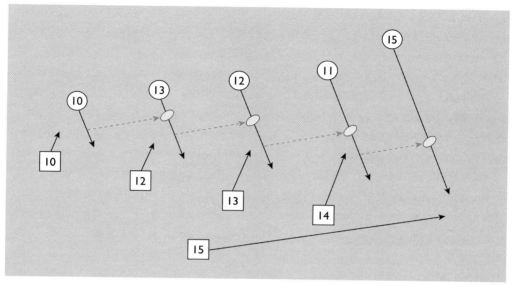

Man-for-man defence *The full-back covers his opposite number, who comes outside the attacking wing to make the extra man. If he has a good understanding with his right-wing, the full-back may prefer to tackle the attacking left-wing, leaving the attacking full-back to his own wing.*

Full-back Anthony Clement of Wales positions himself to tackle Will Carling.

tackle him, pick your spot and go in hard to bring him down.

Drift Defence

This operates mainly from lineout ball. The open-side flanker on the defending side (7) is at the back of the line and closest to the attacking outside-half (10). He runs at the outside-half, leaving his own outside-half to move out and take the inside-centre. Each member of the defending back division drifts across to take the next man in the line. Even if the attacking full-back (15) makes the extra man, he will be covered.

The defending full-back is left free to provide additional cover behind his back-line.

If an attacker breaches the defence, the full-back may be called upon to tackle. He must be unbeatable. No matter how he does it, he must bring his man to the ground. Timing is vital. Go in hard, drive through, hang on tight and bring him down.

Tackling practice is essential. Work hard on this aspect of your game. Speed and positional sense get you to your man. Timing of the tackle makes it really effective. Strength and tenacity do the rest.

Defensive Positions

Stick to a pattern. Divide the pitch into thirds.

Back Third – play will be close to the 22-metre line. The full-back stands 15–20 metres behind his back division. His exact

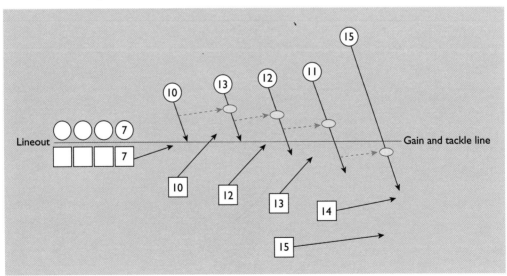

Drift defence Full-back stays behind his back division to provide additional cover.

position will depend on the alignment of his backs but he will usually be directly behind his outside-centre. He is poised to come into the line if a man-for-man defence is called or to provide cover for a drift defence.

Middle Third – the full-back will stand further back and watch the game carefully. Knowledge of opposing teams can be of great help. If you can anticipate what they will do, you can be in a position to counter it.

The best players I ever faced were outside-halves like Gareth Davies of Cardiff and Phil Bennett of Llanelli. Whether playing for their clubs or for Wales, they were brilliant at kicking back into the box for their forwards or using long diagonals to turn me at full-back and make me chase after a rolling ball. By standing further back, I was able to shorten the distance to the ball.

Know your opponents. Identify their tactical kickers. Ease the pressure on yourself by correct positioning.

Front Third – play will be behind the 22-metre line of the opposite team. You are now the full-back of the attacking side but the opposition have the throw-in or the put-in at a scrum. They will secure possession and will almost certainly kick for touch.

Stay closer to the appropriate touch-line to cover the kick in case it misses its mark.

The Back Three

A full-back is no longer a lone defender. He must have a special understanding with his two wings. They join him to form the Back Three. Wings must have pace and anticipation to support their full-back in defensive situations. The trio must work exceptionally well in the back third of the field.

Standard defensive measures involving all three of them should be a regular feature of training sessions. They should build up an interdependence that allows them to improvise when under pressure.

Attack

The full-back can be a key figure in attack. He has a floating role which will keep defending sides guessing. If he varies his attacking play, they will not know when and where he will strike next.

From set positions, there are three main ways in which the full-back may come into the line:

(a) as an extra man to create the overlap
(b) to take the crash ball and breach the defence
(c) as a decoy.

Extra Man

Speed and timing are of the essence. The full-back must not telegraph his intentions to the opposition. He should come into the line at times when he can be most effective. Only practice and experience will tell him when to do this.

On the open-side, he may come in between the outside-centre and the wing to create the overlap. If he has sufficient pace, he may also join the line outside the wing.

From scrum possession, he may come in as an alternative outside-half on the

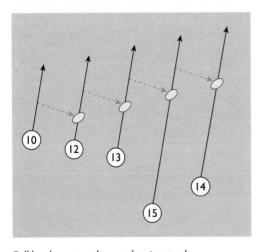

Full-back creates the overlap in attack.

blind-side and take the ball at speed with a wing outside him. If the defence is aligned to cope with the open-side attack, this can be a devastating variation.

Crash Ball

Taking the ball in order to burst through the first line of defence requires speed and power. The angle of running is decisive. Try to wrong-foot the opposition by coming in at an unexpected angle.

Gavin Hastings is a master of the crash ball. He will often take it at top speed and straighten the line of attack to punch a hole in the defence.

Decoy

The full-back who joins the line as a decoy will drag defenders out of position and create space. He may be used to suggest an open-side ploy when the ball will instead go to the blind-side. Or he may be brought into the line to be missed out by a long pass.

Good communication with his back division is again the secret. If a set move is called, the full-back must pick up the signal and be ready to join the line at the designated place. It is vital that one of the wings provides cover for him. As the full-back commits himself to attack, there must be a new last line of defence in case possession is lost.

Counter-attack

The Back Three really come into their own with a counter-attack. When a full-back gathers a ball, he may be in a position to turn defence into attack. He must be supported by the wing who is closest to him.

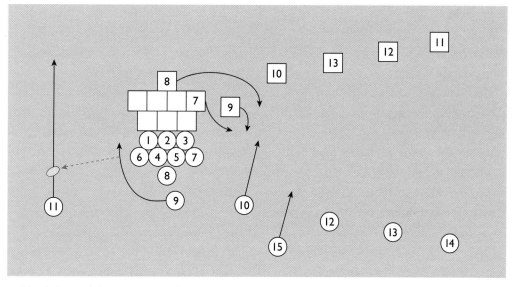

Full-back draws defence to open-side. Scrum-half executes blind-side move.

Counter-attacks from deep positions can be very effective because they are usually unexpected. Andy Irvine was the classic counter-attacker. He had the pace and elusiveness to beat oncoming defenders and the skill to link up with one of his wings.

Serge Blanco was another example of the opportunist full-back with the confidence to run at defences from deep positions.

Flair and ability to improvise are important elements here. The full-back should practise taking a high ball in defence with a wing on hand to support him in the counter-attack. The speed and direction of oncoming opponents will determine which way the full-back decides to break.

If a counter-attack is launched during a game, the full-back and wing will be committed in forward positions. It is up to the other wing to provide cover as auxiliary full-back.

Drop Kicks

This is a scoring option that rarely falls to the full-back. But there are times when he may field a kick out of defence and find himself within range of the goal posts.

Outside-halves like to think of themselves as the drop-kick specialists in a team but it is a valuable weapon in the full-back's armoury as well. When a bad kick out of defence is punished by a drop goal from the full-back, it is a very big psychological blow to the defending side.

Place Kicking

The techniques of place kicking are discussed elsewhere in this book. Its importance in a game cannot be under-rated. Some critics claim that a penalty carries too many points in what is essentially a handling game. They argue that the emphasis on place kicking takes a lot of potential excitement out of a match.

This is not true. Place kicking is an art. A conversion from the touchline in adverse weather conditions or a long-range penalty that sails between the posts can be very thrilling. Paul Thorburn's monster goal kicks for Wales have stayed in the memory along with similar feats by other full-backs.

Place kicking can win games. Every team must therefore have a specialist kicker. This is usually the full-back. If some aspects of his game are weaker, it is still worth playing an outstanding place kicker at full-back.

A full-back who is consistently accurate with his attempts at goal puts an immense pressure on the opposition. When they are in their own half, they know that any infringement of the laws will be punished by the boot. By his very presence in the team, the goal-kicking full-back exerts an influence.

Summary

The full-back must be a good all-round player who works hard to improve every aspect of his game. Defence takes priority. If he is safe and sound in defence, he will boost the confidence of the whole team.

He also has an attacking role to play. How well he does this will depend on his pace, his positional skills, his strength and his stamina. If he sets up a counter-attack, he will need a sense of adventure and an ability to improvise.

The full-back is no longer the lonely man at the back that he once was . He is fully involved in the game from start to finish.

Wing

J. J. Williams

I was born and brought up in the heart of rugby country at Nantyffyllon. Wales has a long and proud association with the game and I absorbed this at an early age. There was never a time when I was not able to watch, discuss, read about and play good rugby. It was my natural habitat. At Maesteg Grammar School and then at Cardiff College of Education, I had the benefit of some excellent coaching. This is vital for any young player. You must have someone who can encourage you, develop your talents properly and give you that bit of inspiration. When I went on to play for Bridgend, my game improved enormously. But it was when I joined Llanelli to be coached by the legendary Carwyn James that my potential was fully realised.

Since Wales has such a remarkable record of turning out superb outside-halves, I was attracted to that position early on. But I eventually came to see that my future lay on the wing. Athletics was also an important part of my life so I had no rest in the close season. I had to maintain my level of fitness throughout the year. In 1971, I was Welsh sprint champion and I went on to represent my country in the Commonwealth Games. My training programme gave me extra speed and stamina that proved invaluable on the rugby field.

Wingers must be supremely fit. It is a position in which any weaknesses can be glaringly exposed. Set yourself high standards and train hard until you reach them. If you wish to become a complete winger, you must be single-minded.

The Complete Wing

It is fairly easy to design the Identikit wing on paper. He must have the following attributes:

(i) Basic speed and acceleration.

(ii) Ability to beat a man.

(iii) Stamina.

(iv) Strength in the tackle.

(v) Safe pair of hands.

(vi) Flair.

Like all three-quarters, of course, he must also have good anticipation and an instinctive sense of positioning. These are the qualities needed and the players who have had them come in all shapes and sizes. Gerald Davies of Wales was a short and slight will-o'-the-wisp. When he was converted into a winger, David Duckham of England was a big, powerful, surging runner. Grant Batty of New Zealand was tiny but lethal. Paddy Batch of Australia was a huge flying machine.

The most dangerous winger I ever faced was Bryan Williams of the All Blacks. He combined pace and power in a fearsome way. A sturdy man with massive thighs, he could blast through opponents or beat them on either side with a devastating body swerve. Once past his man, he would never be caught from behind. Ironically, it was Bryan Williams who helped to coach the Western Samoan team which inflicted such a shock defeat on Wales in the 1991 World Cup.

Today's wingers are equally varied in physique but the high standards persist. Ieuan Evans, captain of Wales, has an abundance of talent. Rory Underwood's try-scoring records for England speak for themselves. His brother, Tony, may well follow in his vapour-trails. John Kirwan is another New Zealand giant of a wing. Simon Geoghegan's electric pace has been a great boon for Ireland. David Campese is the perfect opportunist. And France seems to be able to turn out an endless stream of wingers with exceptional flair.

Watch the best and learn from them. A complete winger must be as effective in defence as in attack. He must also be able to produce that touch of magic when it is most needed. Given the chance, a good winger is a potential match-winner.

Attack

Real pace can test any defence so the wing must be a flyer. The classic try for a wing results from a quick transfer along the three-quarter line that puts him clear of his man.

This may still happen at school or junior level but it is a very rare occurrence in first-class rugby. Defences are too well-organised for such a standard movement to succeed. A wing will only get that kind of space from second or third phase possession, when a defence is caught out of position.

For a winger to be put outside his

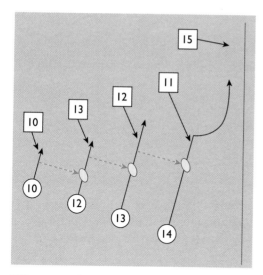

Winger makes outside break *More likely to occur from second or third-phase movements when the defence had been sucked in and the cover weakened.*

man, there must be some midfield ploy. This usually involves the intrusion into the line of the full-back or the blind-side wing to create the overlap. Straight running and a swift transfer of the ball are essential or the wing will be squeezed too close to the touchline.

If you are the blind-side wing, you may come into the back line to act as an extra man or as a decoy. You must have the speed to be in the right place at the right time.

In order to catch the opposition by surprise, leave your intrusion into the line to the last moment.

Wingers do not always get quality ball so they must be able to make the most of

any possession. They should be able to create space for themselves by an injection of pace, by a body swerve or by a side-step off either foot. Even the best defenders can be beaten by a sudden change of direction.

Do not surrender possession. If there is no way through, go hard into the tackle and try to stay on your feet until support comes. Once you have released the ball to your colleague, get straight back into the action.

The chip kick is a potent weapon for any wing but it must be practised carefully. It must also be used in moderation and at the right moment. A wing who kicks ahead every time he gets the ball will never take a defence unawares. You should only use the chip ahead when you are about to be smothered by the defence. Do not yield possession in this way unless you can put real pressure on the opposition. A kick which bounces just over the try-line gives you a good chance against the wing or full-back who has to turn first.

If your pack does not win regular possession, or the midfield has an off-day, you may have a meagre supply of ball. Force your way into the game by foraging for the ball. Utilise your speed to the best advantage by going behind the back line to join in the movement on the opposite side of the field. If you simply wait, the ball may never come.

The inimitable David Campese of Australia.

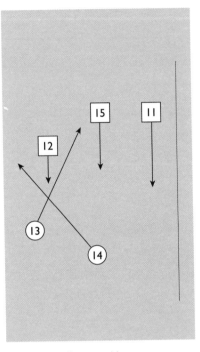

Wing cuts in from touchline to execute scissors with centre and defeat the cover.

Scissors with centre to defeat the cover.

Positioning is another art that must be mastered. It is another way to create a little more space. You must have a good understanding with the midfield players and be attuned to the length and strength of their passes. A long pass may release you to go outside your man. A short one, taken at full speed, may send you through the smallest gap. If you can position yourself correctly, the inside pass taken on the burst near the line, is always a threat.

You must also choose the correct angle of attack. Heavy cover sweeping across the field can often be pierced by a scissors

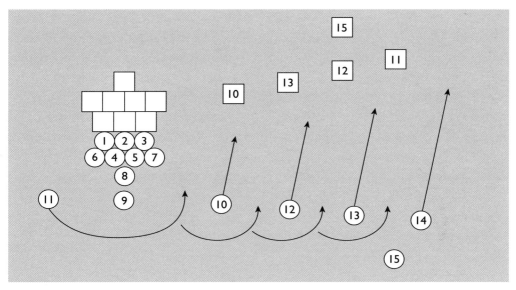

Blind-side wing comes into movement to take inside pass from fly-half near the try-line, or to act as extra man on the loop.

or a reverse pass which alters the line of attack. The wing must know by instinct when to go inside his centre.

Counter-attack

This requires confidence, fitness and sheer flair. The wing who gathers the loose kick ahead is sometimes in a position to launch an audacious counter-attack from a deep position. The French are the past masters of this and the effect on an opposition can be demoralising as they may yield enormous territorial advantage – if not points.

One of the finest tries ever scored at Cardiff Arms Park was the one which set alight the famous 1973 game between the Barbarians and the All Blacks. Phil Bennett gathered a kick ahead deep in his 22-metre area and initiated a movement which went the length of the field and ended with Gareth Edwards hurling himself across the opposition line. Such a try could never be rehearsed. It was spontaneous magic. It came from individual flair and collective commitment.

When a wing collects a ball in a deep position, he must have the confidence to elude the approaching attackers and set up a counter-attack. Be careful not to get stranded. You must link up with supporting players who can continue the play.

Opportunities for such a counterattack may not come along very often. When they do, seize on them.

Defence

Every winger has a preference for right or left but the complete player should be able to acquit himself well on either side of the field. This will certainly increase his chances of being selected at representative level because he can be considered for two positions instead of simply one.

The left-wing usually has to do more defending than the right. Most scrum-halves and outside-halves are right-footed and will therefore put in tactical kicks as the play moves towards the right-hand touchline. The left-wing is often very much under fire.

Practise retrieving the diagonal kick ahead which lands in your own 22-metre area. Collect, turn and kick to touch. Two attackers will put you under pressure.

The right-wing will also have to deal

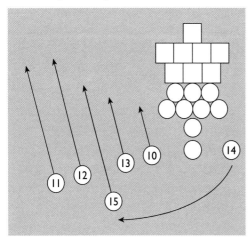

Wing moving to full-back position when own full-back is committed in a forward position.

with the kick ahead in the same way. The bounce of the ball may determine what he does. If it is awkward to collect, he may have no option but to kick to touch. A kinder bounce may give him marginally more time in which to beat the attackers before clearing the ball. Practise eluding opponents and then kicking.

A wing must also act as an alternative full-back when his own full-back joins the line as an extra man or gets caught up in the play.

Wingers must therefore be able to catch a high ball and put it into touch with the consistency of a full-back. Regular kicking and catching practice is thus mandatory. The wing must also develop the positional sense of a full-back so that he is in the right place to deal with kicks ahead.

Sound tackling is a key ingredient. You must be able to tackle firmly and bring your man down. When your opposite number gets the ball in a three-quarter movement, try to force him towards the touchline so that he has only one way to run. You can then tackle him into touch and stop any chance of second-phase possession for the attackers.

When an extra man comes into the line, wingers may be faced with a two-to-one situation. Move in swiftly to tackle the extra man or he will be through the gap. Try to hit him before he can pass the ball to his own wing.

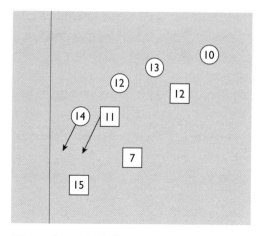

Winger forces the ball-carrier towards the touch-line before tackling him.

If the extra man has the time to draw you before passing to his wing, do not commit yourself to the tackle. Shadow the extra man until he passes the ball then move out to bring down the wing.

How and when to tackle will depend

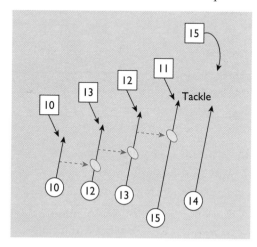

Man-for-man defence *Winger in man-to-man defence, coming in to tackle extra man to abort an attack.*

how near your line the attack is. If your opposite number is haring for the corner flag and you tackle him from the side, his impetus may take him over the line. Only a crash tackle into touch will save a try in this situation.

Another tight situation arises when the opposition have the put-in at a scrum five metres from your line. The blind-side wing must be on the line itself to guard against a move that involves scrum-half, back-row or wing. The attackers will use their weight and power to drive for the line. Do not wait for them to come. Move forward and drive into the tackle.

As a general rule, go hard and fast into any tackle. Bring down your man before he can build up any speed. You then cut down his thinking time and ability to manoeuvre.

Summary

Master all the elements of the game if you wish to be a complete winger. Work closely with your centres and full-back so that you build up an instinctive under-standing. Practise beating a defender in limited space as you go for the try-line. Use the full range of your abilities. Beat him with speed, a swerve, a side-step, a hand-off, a kick ahead or a feigned kick ahead which will force him to turn.

Practise both attacking and defensive

Lifted by the crowd, Rory Underwood races to score another vital try.

manoeuvres until they become second nature to you. Value spontaneity. The best wingers are those with the imagination to do the unexpected and to change the face of the game with a burst of brilliance. Welsh rugby was supreme in the 1970s and I was lucky enough to be part of its success. We played an expansive game that was grounded on excellent teamwork. But individual flair was encouraged and the enterprising wingers in those teams made a scintillating contribution to the Triple Crowns and Gland Slams.

The game will always need wingers of such calibre.

Centre

David Duckham

During the evolution of the game since the last war, there was a long period when three-quarter play – and back play, in general – was dictated more by a contrasting individualism that involved exemplary skills than by any definable style of play across the board.

There was something of a revolution in 1965 when the predatory open-side wing-forwards (later re-christened flankers) were not allowed to break their binding at the back of the scrum until the ball was heeled. Other law changes followed which were to have profound effects – the statutory 10-metre gap between lineout and fly-half; and a radical restriction on touch-kicking outside your own 22-metre area. Rugby football was trying to legislate for greater creativity. Some of these changes were designed to liberate those behind the scrum, notably the centres and the wing three-quarters.

The other major influence on the game was the coaching explosion in the mid-1960s, conceived in England and pioneered in Wales by Ray Williams, who was undoubtedly inspired by the former New Zealand coach Fred Allen. A sublime period, from the late 1960s to the early 1970s, saw the realisation of a dream which belonged to that doyen of coaching, the late Carwyn James. It was he who steered the 1971 British Lions to their only victory in a Test series against the All Blacks on the latter's hallowed ground. Carwyn James had a vision which added new dimensions to three-quarter play – the introduction of an attacking full-back into the line and the notion of counter-attacking from deep positions.

The broadening of three-quarter play enabled centres to be far more creative until, that is, coaching took a real stranglehold at club level. Styles of play then tended to revert to a stereotype which was all too predictable. There was a whole array of set-piece ploys and pre-planned moves outside the scrum. Before the changes in the laws, space was so confined that centres had to survive on instinct, flair and opportunism. Individual skills were paramount. Later, however, pre-match planning through squad sessions and an obsession with highly organised defences created a general stalemate. Flair and individual brilliance were suppressed to the point of regression. Percentage rugby came to the fore and, in many ways, has remained ever since.

The Great Players

Notwithstanding the general decline in standards, which was nowhere more noticeable than in midfield, there have been a number of supremely gifted individuals who have graced the field with distinction in the post-war years. The archetypal English centre was Jeff Butterfield, all hips and swagger. His deceptive long stride created many an outside break. Butterfield was aided by the direct running and bludgeoning power of his long-time partner, W. P. C. Davies.

In Wales, meanwhile, another renowned partnership was already an institution in the 1950s. Jack Matthews and Bleddyn Williams both came from the famous Cardiff stable. Matthews was the straight man, feared for his crash-tackling, and Williams was the twinkle-toed wizard. Described by his contemporary, Carwyn James, as 'the most gifted of centres', Bleddyn Williams was a genius who could side-step through any defence and accelerate away at breathtaking speed. He was certainly the finest centre of his generation. Gerald Davies, better known as a wing three-quarter, originally played as a centre with something of the Williams magic.

During the 1960s, one South African centre in particular caused havoc in opposition defences. John Gainsford was big, strong and fast. In sharp contrast were his two Western Province colleagues, Eben Olivier and F. du T. Roux. Olivier was the stylish touch player while the diminutive Roux was a fearless crash-tackler.

New Zealand centres in the post-war era tended to favour the battering-ram technique, as exemplified by Ian MacRae in the 1960s. But the All Blacks did make a real contribution to the development of midfield play with players such as Bruce Robertson. Those who saw the epic 1973 match at Cardiff Arms Park between the Barbarians and the All Blacks will know that Bruce Robertson played a major part in both of Grant Batty's tries. A centre in the classic mould, who liked to carry the ball in both hands, Robertson's long stride and high knee action made him extremely difficult to put down. He was succeeded by the slightly built Steve Pokere who had strength, tremendous acceleration and the ability to wriggle out of tackles in the tightest of situations.

In France, where there is great emphasis on adventurous back play, there have been many exceptional centres over the years. The best known in my time was Jo Maso – or Maso the Magician. He deceived opponents with sleight-of-hand (now you see it, now you don't) and with subtle changes of pace. Other masters of the midfield were Jean Trillo, Jean-Pierre Lux, Claude Dourthe and Roland Betranne. And the list goes on.

Probably the finest exponent of centre play, in terms of all-round ability and sheer versatility, has been Michael Gibson, a simply remarkable player whose illustrious international career lasted sixteen seasons. Though capped by Ireland in almost every position behind the scrum, it was as a centre that he excelled and achieved worldwide renown, producing the very best exam-ples of ball skills, tactical awareness and vision, strength, agility, speed and stamina. Mike Gibson was truly the complete rugby player.

As the game moves forward, and with increasing positional specialisation, I am not sure we shall see the likes of Gibson again on the international stage. That is a great loss to the game of rugby.

Then and Now

The argument which rages from time to time in every clubhouse bar is how well the great players of the past compare with their successors. Would Maso, Williams, Gibson and their like have survived in the modern game? The answer must be yes. Yesterday's centres were equally skilful and, in certain areas, even more proficient than today's players. Indeed, a period of stagnation has been apparent in recent years. Midfield play is often very dull.

However, the face of the game has certainly altered, along with styles of play and attitudes. The sheer pace of rugby at international level has speeded up to the point where there is almost no time or space for the individual flair of yesteryear to show through.

Past masters who relied on space in which to manoeuvre would be largely ineffective in today's congested midfield, except in certain secondary phases of attack. Even those whose hallmark was pure instinct and a flair for the unex-pected would be nullified more often than not by the superior organisation of defences. Second and third lines of defence now arrive with alarming speed to give strength in depth.

Today's players are much fitter and probably faster because the physical preparation for international rugby is much more intense and comprehensive. Even dietary considerations now play a much more significant part in the pre-match build-up as players seek to conserve energy and maximise physical performance on the day.

Role of the Centre

Despite the vagaries and relative mediocrity of midfield play in the modern game, the basic role of the centre has not changed over the years. His function is to:

(i)   Provide rapid and effective possession to the wing three-quarters.
(ii) Generate an efficient and smooth-running back line.
(iii) Defend against all manner of attack.

A fly-half will not always distribute good ball and a split-second decision may be required to convert bad or indifferent possession into something more positive and creative. Kick, pass, run at the opposition with or without a set-piece move – these are the options in attack. Choosing the right option under extreme pressure is the mark of a good centre.

Midfield Partnerships

These are just as important in the modern game as they have ever been. However skilled or versatile an individual player may be, there is nothing more effective than a pair of centres combining in perfect harmony while showing a visible contrast in their styles of play. A keen understanding of each other's strengths and weaknesses is a key component of the ideal partnership. Mutual awareness and a sense of natural anticipation of individual actions are also important elements.

Though not a definitive example, my own relationship with fellow-centre John Spencer during our England and Barbarian matches contained these ingredients and they were patently founded upon and moulded by our close friendship off the field. Above all else, our respective styles of play were compatible – John was the hard, straight, determined runner and I tried to exploit the openings which he created. Our success was based on total commitment in support of each other's actions.

Ray Gravell and David Richards were equally effective for Wales in the 1970s, the master of the crash-ball and the dazzling artist. It is a pity they played together so few times because they were a perfect combination. The outstanding partnership in today's game has been that of Will Carling and Jeremy Guscott for England. They provide an interesting contrast. Carling, the England captain, is never afraid to take on the whole opposition with his direct running, though he does not always seek to provide the

David Duckham bemuses the defender with his combined swerve and dummy in the famous Barbarians v. All Blacks game in 1973.

appropriate release for the eminently dangerous Guscott, whose grace, speed and elusiveness are a joy to behold.

Centre Positions

There are two positional options which centres can adopt on the field of play:

(i)   Inside and outside.
(ii) Left and right.

In the southern hemisphere – notably in Australia and New Zealand – a centre must be either an inside-centre or an outside-centre. The fly-half is called the first five-eighth and the inside-centre is known as the second five-eighth. It is the outside-centre, therefore, who is recognised as the true centre three-quarter.

The All Blacks' style in this department was distinctive in my time. The second five-eighth played as a cross between a fly-half and a centre, and he was certainly a contact player. Ian MacRae was a case in point. The tactic of using the second five-eighth to pierce the first line of defence became commonplace and thus predictable. However, the ploy was used to good effect because whenever the second five-eighth was tackled, the superior strength and technique of the All Blacks in ruck and maul almost invariably secured second-phase possession. Greater attention to defence largely negated this type of initiative in later years with the ball carrier often being driven backwards in the tackle.The tactical predictability of using an inside and outside formation is such that the other option is usually preferred in the British Isles and France. Very few players could perform equally well as inside and outside-centres, though two obvious exceptions to this were Mike Gibson and John Dawes, his captain and co-centre on the 1971 victorious British Lions tour of New Zealand. If centres play left and right respectively, they each have the chance to be inside and outside.

Lines of Running

It was Carwyn James who first pointed out that rugby was a game of angles. One of the most important disciplines to master concerns angles or lines of running, both in attack and in defence. There is no finer sight than the swift transfer of the ball along the three-quarter line but there is always a tendency

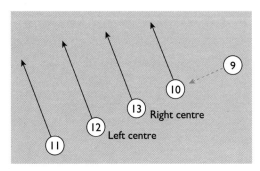

Left and right centres *Back line with left and right centres.*

to run diagonally towards the touchline rather than straight upfield. This is because the three-quarters are aligned at a 45 degree angle to the touchline at the outset. The wing quickly runs out of lateral space.

A conscious effort must be made to straighten the line of attack. The crucial figure is the fly-half. The direction of his running will guide those outside him. Normally, he will accelerate on to a pass

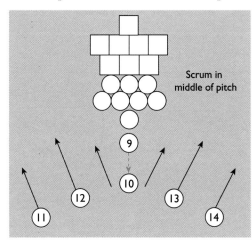

Lines of running *The fly half's direction will guide those outside him*

from his scrum-half and then release it. Another option, increasingly used today, is for the fly-half to take the ball almost at a standstill. He will then time a static pass to the inside-centre – or even the outside-centre – who is thus able to receive the ball at speed and choose a straighter line of running.

Occasionally, even an inside-centre may take the ball in a standing position for a quick movement to his midfield partner. Both these plays are designed to allow more flexibility in attack, enabling ball transfer to take place further away from the opposition back line. This, added to a deep alignment, will allow a centre more time to determine whether to pass, kick or take on his opposite number.

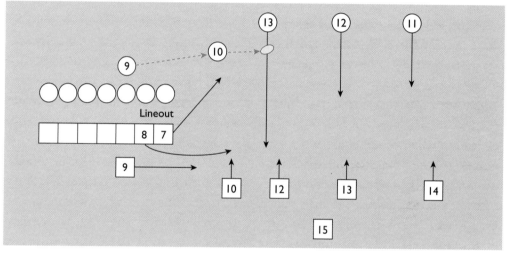

Back line with fly-half giving static pass to inside-centre who then runs straight.

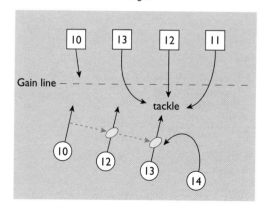

A breakdown in a deeply aligned back-line.

Creativity and variation form the essence of midfield play. The French have always had the courage to align deeply. I use the word 'courage' because there had always been a marked resistance to the idea, the main fear being that any particular three-quarter movement will not reach the advantage line and so be deemed to have failed. Or will it? Just how important it is that a movement crosses this line before any breakdown occurs is debatable.

The most likely interruption is when

the ball carrier is tackled. Good support from the other three-quarters and from the forwards should ensure that possession is retained. But there is a psychological element here as well. The principal objective of three-quarter play is to carry the ball nearer to the opposition try-line. A breakdown behind the advantage line will be very discouraging to the forwards, who will begrudge the threat to such hard-won possession. Also, it is much easier to run upfield in support than to trudge back to rescue a try-line.

Alignment

A deep formation will often fail if the ball is transferred along the line too quickly, because the opposing three-quarters, not committed to man-to-man defence, will simply drift across the field and crowd out the final ball-carrier near the touch-line. The French technique is to straighten their line in attack and delay their pass until they have committed a defender. This does not put the receiver under pressure because the alignment allows vital extra space and time in which to choose the right option.

Correct alignment is vital in defence as well. Defenders must come up in a controlled line. Poor alignment leads to the so-called 'dog-leg' and is easily exploited by a strong-running centre. Even if he does not breach the first line of

defence himself, he should run at the gap in order to interest two defenders. A well-timed pass could then create a gap for the player outside him.

As soon as he has room for manoeuvre, a centre should always be encouraged to take on his opposite number in order to test him. A defender who is slow or weak in the tackle must be exposed and exploited to maximum advantage. Resistance can be examined simply by running directly at a defender. Few players relish the head-on tackle. Velocity gives additional strength to the ball-carrier against a tackler who is made to stand still by the angle of approach.

The ball-carrier must always have the advantage and he should at least be able to ride the impact of the tackle and keep the ball available. A fellow-centre or wing should anticipate the moment of collision and time his approach so that he can take the pass from the tackled player. In today's game, it is crucial to try to stay on your feet in the tackle. The support player must be able to improvise. He may well have to secure possession by snatching it at close quarters from his colleague rather than by taking a conventional pass.

Kicking

All centres must be proficient kickers. The fly-half is often in the best position

Jeremy Guscott, the supreme centre.

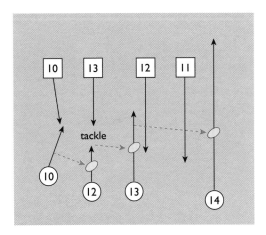

Centre running straight at defender then transferring ball to support player when tackled.

to execute tactical kicks but the role can also fall to the centres.

Grubber kick. The teasing kick along the ground into the area behind the opposition centres. It forces the defence to turn and chase back after an awkwardly bouncing ball. The grubber should be angled so that a centre or wing can run on to it at speed.

Chip kick. The delicate kick over the heads of the opposition midfield can have the same effect. Like the grubber, it is very effective against a defence which comes up too quickly. A chip kick may curb their zeal by a yard or two. It is best used from a scrum. From a line-out, there is a greater risk of defending flankers getting to the target area first and gaining possession.

Diagonal kick. From either of the set-piece situations, a long, raking diagonal kick towards the corner flag can gain considerable territorial advantage. A static pass from the fly-half should give the inside-centre ample time to put in a carefully directed punt. One of the finest exponents of this kick was Paul Dodge, the Leicester and England centre. His left boot was capable of taking play forty yards upfield.

High kick. The up-and-under towards the posts gives both centres a chance to sprint hard in an attempt either to catch the ball themselves, to pressurise the catcher into error, or to tackle him hard and regain possession.

Kicks must be used intelligently. If the wrong option is taken, it is all too easy to squander possession. The risk factor must be assessed by the kicker. His side must have a better than even chance of scoring or getting the ball back again.

Planned Moves

A major legacy of the coaching revolution was the emphasis on planned set-piece three-quarter moves. The need to acquire certain unit skills is obvious but it can be taken to extremes. All sense of enterprise can then be squeezed out of the game. As defences become more organised, there is a common belief that

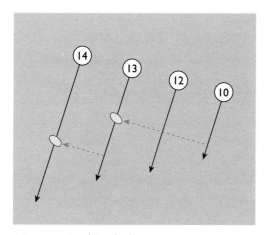

Miss move involving both centres.

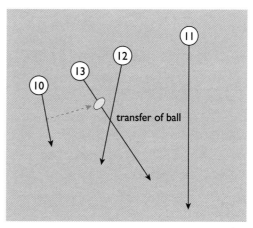

Switch or scissors in midfield.

only sophisticated set-piece moves will break the deadlock. Rehearsed moves certainly have their place but flair and improvisation must not be surrendered.

Set-piece moves should be simple, swiftly executed and must not involve too many players. They need to be practised regularly so that they become smooth and reliable. Certain basic moves should be in the armoury of every team:

Extra Man. The full-back or the blind-side wing comes into the line to create an overlap. They can intrude between or outside the centres.

Decoy. The extra man in the line is only a decoy and is missed out by the ball-carrier when he passes the ball.

Miss move. To transfer the ball more quickly along the line, the fly-half or the inside-centre misses out the player alongside him with a long pass.

Double miss move. This is possible when an extra man comes into the line. Two players are then missed out consecutively by long passes.

Switch or scissors. This effects a sudden change in the angle of attack and can be devastating if timed properly.

Timing is paramount in all cases. Planned moves must have an element of surprise and not be telegraphed. Variation of midfield play should keep the opposition guessing. There must be room for the unusual and unexpected. John Spencer and I occasionally changed places during the match just to confuse the opposition. Anything which will cause a defence to hesitate must be seen as a valuable attacking weapon.

My first international try was based on a classic planned move. From a line-out, the ball was moved left along the three-quarter line. John Spencer, at right-centre, missed me out and passed to Rodney Webb on the wing. Deliberately lying a little closer to me, Webb took the ball at speed and straightened to beat the tackle of his opposite number on the inside. I had time to sprint around him and appear on his left to take the pass he released when he had committed the Irish full-back, Tom Kiernan. Taking the ball at full pace on the halfway line, I had a race for the line with the Irish cover.

Defence

The above move was designed to break the first line of defence and resulted in a try. Apart from the full-back, there was no real secondary cover. Today's defences are much more organised and a centre taking the ball on the overlap in this way would face stronger cover. By the same token, he could rely on much better close support. What the move does demonstrate is the importance of work off the ball. The outside-centre, who is missed out by the pass, gets into a position where the movement can continue.

Defence is a prime part of a centre's job. He must be firm in the tackle and have the physical presence to ruck and maul. Forward mobility is such that a centre may well have to tackle the biggest members of the opposition pack.

Good communication lies at the heart of defence. Centres must know who is marking whom. They must have an excellent understanding with their outside-half. Whether they use man-to-man or drift defence, they must come up in a solid line that leaves the opposition with no enticing gaps. When a side loses the ball in broken play, its back-line must be able to take instant defensive action.

Centre three-quarters should follow the same guidelines in defence as in attack:

   (i)   Work together.
  (ii)   Be alert.
 (iii)   Be adaptable.
 (iv)   Develop your physical presence.
  (v)   Perfect your timing.

Scrum-Half and Outside-Half

Les Cusworth

Help and support at an early age are vital. I owe so much to my father, Cec, a Yorkshire miner. He brought us up to love sport and encouraged my rugby career every inch of the way. When I went to Normanton Grammar School, I was coached by Alan Jubb, who also had a massive influence on me. I was a scrum-half in those days. His attitude was simple. 'Run it,' he would say. 'Why kick when you can put it through the hands?' That advice is as relevant in the modern game as it was then.

I moved to outside-half in the sixth form and knew I had found my true position. But the experience at scrum-half gave me a real understanding of that role as well. My senior rugby was played for Wakefield then Moseley, but it was Leicester which transformed my game. Chalkie White was an inspirational coach. At my first training session, he made me do thirty minutes of tackling practice with the forwards. Having exposed my weaknesses, he set about repairing them. His philosophy was, 'I know what you can do. Let's work on what you can't do.' This practical approach paid rich dividends for me.

Every player needs a Chalkie White, a coach you can trust and respect. He was my mentor and he was full of wise comments on the game. One of his favourite remarks was, 'A player who doesn't make a mistake doesn't make a decision.' That applies particularly to the half-backs because they must both be leading decision-makers in any team.

Scrum-Half

The scrum-half is the link between the forwards and the backs. It is the key position for keeping the game alive. There is no respite for a scrum-half. He is totally involved throughout the game. He must be an all-action player with the stamina to keep going until the final whistle.

The list of great scrum-halves is endless. It includes little Scotch terriers like Roy Laidlaw and Gary Armstrong; big, strong men like Terry Holmes or Nick Farr-Jones, who can act as a ninth forward if occasion demands; lethal predators like David Kirk or Pierre Berbizier; and a one-off genius like Gareth Edwards. On their day, they were match-winners.

I was lucky enough to play at club or international level outside such scrum-halves as Nick Youngs, Steve Kenney and Nigel Melville. All three were durable, reliable and highly inventive. The best scrum-half with whom I played was Jerome Gallion of France, a tiny man with a speedy and accurate pass as well as electric acceleration from a standing start. He created space for the outside-half. That is crucial.

Passing

A scrum-half must have a good service. Its elements are:

(i) Speed.
(ii) Accuracy.
(iii) Length.

Fast hands are essential. A scrum-half must be able to get the ball out quickly from all situations. In scooping the ball

up from the base of the scrum, his action should be kept to a minimum. Players who need a long wind-up before they pass will never make good scrum-halves. They are much more likely to be caught in possession. Even a second's delay in getting the ball away may be critical. Work on developing your speed of pass. Eliminate backswing.

Accuracy is also imperative. The swiftest pass is useless if it does not find its target. Half-backs must always practise together so that they build up a complete understanding. A scrum-half should be able to find his partner with a pass at all times, whether from set-pieces or in broken play.

Length is not as important as speed or accuracy. Too long a service may indeed be a disadvantage because it cuts down the space in which the back-line can operate. At the same time, however, a pass should be long enough to put an outside-half clear of immediate danger. This is especially the case when a team has a put-in or throw-in near its own line. The scrum-half must be able to give a pass that allows his outside-half (or full-back) time to put in a relieving kick to touch. In this situation, the speed, accuracy and length of his service will be put under pressure.

Passing Practice

Pass from the ground in a one-movement

sweep. Watch the ball and get your body in a correct position. You need a wide leg span with the weight on your back foot. The other foot will point in the direction where the ball will go.

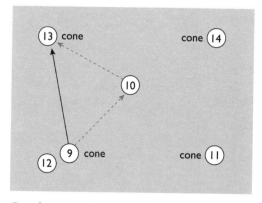

Passing exercise, *using four cones and involving scrum-half, outside-half and four other players. Scrum-half runs in clockwise direction.*

Passing is not a hand action. It is a whole body movement. Always practise with a partner so that you have a target. The scrum-half will handle the ball more often than any other member of the team. In attack and defence, he will need a safe pair of hands. Work to develop that safety.

Place four cones 25 metres apart to form a square. A player will be stationed at each corner. The outside-half is in the centre of the square. The scrum-half picks the ball up from the ground beside one cone, passes to the outside-half then runs to the next cone. The outside-half will return the ball to the player at the next corner so that it is on the ground for the approaching scrum-half to pick up and pass.

Alter the direction of the run so that you are passing to your left at each corner. The outside-half may vary his position so that length and angle of pass need to be adjusted. This is not just a passing exercise. It is good fitness training for a scrum-half who will be constantly racing to the breakdown to get the ball away.

Dive Pass

The dive pass is most useful when the scrum-half is under great pressure. He will get the ball away faster and make himself a more difficult target for the harrying forwards. The correct technique needs to be mastered. Keep your back foot behind the ball. Place your hands on either side of the ball. Transfer your weight and pivot over the front foot so that you can dive forward and up towards the target. Sweep the ball away and dispatch it with a flick of the wrists.

The dive pass looks spectacular but should only be used when necessary. A scrum-half should try to stay on his feet when he passes and thus remain in the game. A dive pass takes him momentarily out of the action. Players who give a dive pass from every set-piece are no threat to an opposing back-row who simply head

Michael Bradley of Ireland with a perfect dive pass. Number 8, Brian Robinson, watches with approval.

straight for the outside-half when the ball is whipped out.

Practise the dive pass regularly. Place four balls in line five metres apart. Run to the first ball, pick it up and give a dive pass to another player who is in position. Recover quickly and turn to pick up the next ball to dive pass in the opposite direction to another support player. Repeat the exercise with the next two balls.

To add variety, give a dive pass with the first ball, then a standing pass, then another dive pass and so on. Players who receive the balls will return them to their original position on the line so that the practice is continuous.

Pivot Pass

This is a variation that allows the scrum-half to exploit his stronger hand in a pass. Most scrum-halves are right-handed and will thus find it easier to pass from right to left. They spin the ball off their right or bottom hand. From a lineout on the left touchline, some players prefer to take the ball and pivot to the left so that they can use their right hands to control the release of the ball. They will thus be passing with their back to the opposition.

Positioning is critical in such a case. The scrum-half must stand a few feet to the infield of the catcher and face slightly

Robert Jones of Wales, master of the pivot pass.

towards the touchline. As the ball comes, he pivots on the right foot until his left foot faces the target. Then he gets the ball away.

In some situations, the pivot pass is the only option and scrum-halves must learn to pivot in either direction. This pass will be marginally slower than the others so the outside-half must adjust his position accordingly. As with all other passes, practice makes perfect.

Attack

Every time he gets the ball, the scrum-half is faced with a choice. He can pass it out, kick, make a break or feed it back to the forwards. The only way to make the correct decision is to be aware of what is happening all around you. This will only come from playing experience. Decisions will be made in a split-second. They must be automatic.

Good communication is everything. The scrum-half must be communicating with his forwards and his backs through-out the game. He does this with words and with pre-arranged signals so that everyone knows what is happening at set-pieces. Every time there is a break-down, the scrum-half is able to speak to the forwards. He should take this opportunity to encourage, exhort and direct.

Code words should be simple and easy to understand. Signals should be clear yet concealed from the opposition. Many players use hands on their hips to mean one thing, hands by their side to mean another, hands behind their back to signal something else again. A hand brushed through the hair or the pulling up of socks in a given order are other easy signals.

Scrums

It is important to give signals to the forwards before they go down in the scrum. They must know if they are going for a push-over try, a quick heel or a back-row ploy. It is easier for the scrum-half to communicate with the three-quarter line because he can always give a signal to them behind his back.

The classic attacking situation is a scrum in the middle of the pitch on the opposition 22-metre line. The scrum-half signals quick-channel ball to the forwards. The outside-half can go to the right, to the left or attempt a drop kick. He will make that decision and signal accordingly.

From the same scrum, of course, the scrum-half can break in either direction himself, chip ahead or link up with his back-row in a pre-arranged ploy. A typi-

Richard Hill puts the ball in during a club game for Bath, watched carefully by his opposite number.

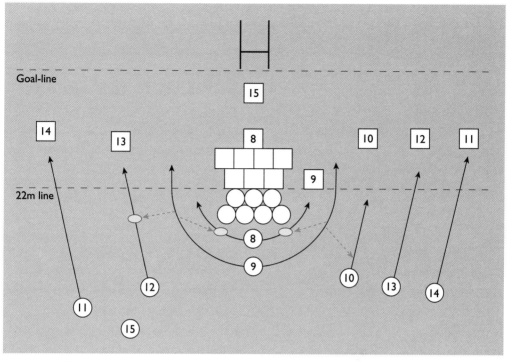

Scrum in middle of opposition 22-metre line. Options available to scrum-half and number 8.

cal example of the latter tactic is for the scrum to break wide and feed the supporting flanker, who will in turn give it to the number 8. When the thrust is halted, the scrum-half is in position to take the second-phase ball and whip it out to his backs.

A scrum in an attacking position near a touchline gives the scrum-half the option of using the blind-side. A quick ball will allow him to break and either pass to the wing or feed his back-row again.

It is important to try as many variations as possible so that the defence is never sure what is going to happen next. Defending back-lines will come up much quicker from a scrum than a lineout. A chip kick behind the advancing line can also be used but only if there is a good chance of scoring or of securing possession again.

It is more difficult to use signals for rucks and mauls though a shouted code-word will tell the forwards when to drive forward and when to give the ball back. As always every situation must be practised regularly so that there is an excellent rapport between a scrum-half and his pack.

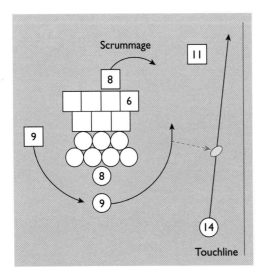

Scrum near touchline *Scrum-half goes on blind-side run and feeds wing.*

Lineouts

It is much easier for the scrum-half to communicate with his pack when they are all standing up. On the throw-in, he will indicate the jumper with a signal or a code-word or a set of numbers. He will position himself a few paces from the line and near the jumper so that he can take and give the ball at speed.

Back divisions always prefer the ball sooner rather than later and the quickest ball comes from a lineout. The scrum-half will therefore usually launch an attack by getting the ball out but there are other options. A long throw taken by a jumper at the back of the line may be knocked down to a scrum-half who loops to the open and links up with his back-line.

Another option for the alert scrum-half is to take the ball at the front of the lineout as long as it is thrown in straight and travels the minimum five metres.

The high kick is another attacking option for a scrum-half who can make it hang high in the air in front of the opposition posts so that his centres can run on to it.

Tap Penalty

If a tap penalty is called, the scrum-half is the key player who initiates the pre-planned move. He must secure the ball as quickly as possible and take the penalty before the opposition can organise its defence. A typical ploy is for the scrum-half to tap the ball to himself, pass to a forward nearby who remains stationary, loop around him to take the

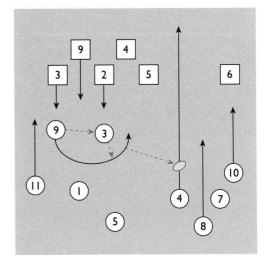

Tap penalty as described above.

The all-round scrum-half right-footed Robert Jones kicks equally well with his left foot when required.

ball then pass it to a player who is coming through on the burst to punch a hole in the defence.

Defence

The only true test of a scrum-half is to watch him playing behind a beaten pack. His defensive game will be put under severe examination. He will have to tackle, cover and tidy up a lot of bad ball from his forwards.

His principal task at a scrum is to police his opposite number when the latter has the put-in. Close down his options and apply pressure. Harry him when the ball comes out and run on to harry the outside-half.

The scrum-half will have to tackle big forwards who come at him from the back-row of a scrum or who burst through a lineout. Go in hard and firm before they can build up any momentum. If the opposition has a scrum five metres from the line, you have to be especially alert. This is the perfect position for a back-row ploy. Try to snuff it out at source.

You must be able to kick with either foot under extreme pressure. Opposition forwards may close on you from a set-piece or in broken play and your only

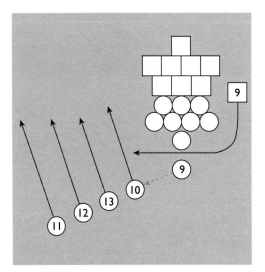

Defending scrum-half as ball comes out on opposing side and is passed down the line.

option is to put in a relieving kick to touch. Practise doing this with both feet while being harried by other players. When you have very little room to work in, make sure you give the ball a sharp trajectory so that it is not charged down. Most of all, make sure it goes into touch. Do not give the opposition a chance to counter-attack from a bad kick out of defence.

Summary

If you work hard on every aspect of your game, most of what you do will become instinctive. But there must also be room for improvisation. A scrum-half must be spontaneous and exploit the chances that come. Make a break and you become a problem to the opposition. They have to worry about you. Be an efficient link between the forwards and the backs but keep an eye open for that opportunity to make a break.

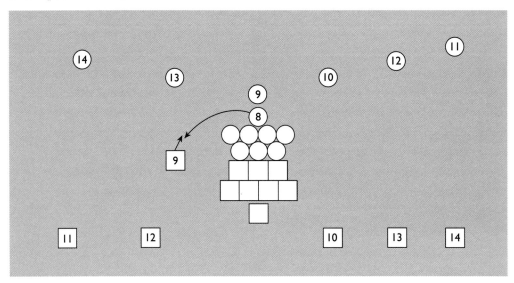

Scrum near line *Defending scrum-half takes out number 8 in attacking ploy.*

Outside-Half

Like his partner, the outside-half has a vital role as a facilitator. He must get his back-line going. He must be able to handle heavy responsibilities and to take a series of split-second decisions. The half-back unit is highly visible and highly involved in any game. A wide range of abilities is required from both players.

British rugby has been blessed with some superb outside-halves over the years. Barry John was a sprite who could ghost through a defence. The diminutive Phil Bennett, his successor in the Welsh team, was a perfectionist who honed every aspect of his game. When the tall and stylish Gareth Davies took over, his tactical kicking was exemplary. Ollie Campbell of Ireland was another master of the boot. His rival, Tony Ward, was a tough, busy, bustling player who was quite fearless. Grant Fox of New Zealand, though criticised for over-use of the high kick, is an extremely efficient fly-half who is quite capable of making a telling break. Naas Botha of South Africa is another superb kicker who can run the ball when the opportunity comes.

During my long playing career at outside-half, I saw many changes in the game. The pace increased, the intensity deepened and the coaching improved enormously. Defences were better organised and outside-halves were given less time and space in which to operate. The fly-half of today must be able to tackle. It is no longer a position where a prima donna can show off his skills in attack and simply play a shadowing role in defence. Forwards are highly mobile. They love to run at the half-backs. And a fly-half will now be called upon to tackle his opposite number. Like the scrum-half, he will be in the thick of it from start to finish.

A complete outside-half must therefore have many attributes:

(i) Safe hands.
(ii) Speed and acceleration.
(iii) Ability to kick well with either foot.
(iv) Capacity to make instant decisions.
(v) Positional skill.
(vi) Anticipation.
(vii) Prowess as a tackler.

Since the fly-half will catch and pass the ball endlessly throughout a game, he must practise with his half-back partner until they function as a smooth unit; and he must develop a similar understanding with his midfield.

Place four balls in a line fifteen metres apart. The scrum-half stands near the first ball. The outside-half is in position to take it as he moves left. When he takes the pass from the scrum-half, he gives it to the centre outside him then goes on a diagonal run to his right. The scrum-half

John Rutherford of Scotland sets his back-line in motion.

runs to the next ball and passes it to the outside-half, who is now moving to the right. He will catch and pass to the other centre then go on a diagonal run to the left, linking up once more with the other centre.

This exercise gives the outside-half practice of taking the ball from alternate directions and of switching the angle of attack quickly. All four players get good handling practice and fitness training. Vary the length of pass between the half-backs and between the outside-half and his centres. Familiarity will breed confidence.

Attack

The main task of the outside-half is to get the three-quarters on the move. The more pairs of hands the ball has to travel through, the more chances for error. The miss move does not just confuse a defence. It gets the ball more swiftly out to the wing. The quickest way for the outside-half to get the ball to the wing, of course, is to attack down the blind-side when the opportunity presents. Only one pass is then needed.

The quality of possession will determine the options. An outside-half who gets good, quick ball has fractionally more thinking time to make the right decision.

Scrums

Never squander good possession. Call the move before the scrum goes down and make sure everyone knows what is happening. If it is a conventional three-quarter movement with a speedy transfer of the ball to the wing, take the ball on the move, accelerate and draw your man, then give a good pass to your inside-centre. Loop behind the back-line to offer support and continue the move or to be on hand at any breakdown.

From a scrum deep in the opposition half, you can run, pass or kick. If the scrum is infield, you will also have a choice of going in either direction. Pick the most effective way to strike for the line. Experience will guide you.

If the defending three-quarters do not come up in a line, go for the gap and make the break or the half-break. This takes the pressure off your own centres and gets them through the first line of defence. It will also make the opposition treat you with respect. Make them worry about you.

If a three-quarter movement is called, get the ball out quickly so that the midfield have room to manoeuvre. A

simple but effective ploy is the loop. The outside-half passes to his inside-centre then loops around him to take the ball as the extra man in the line and so create an overlap. A variation is for the outside-half to pass and loop behind the two centres so that he can collect the ball again and set up the wing.

Standard midfield ploys are described elsewhere in this book. Remember not to over-complicate. The ball then has to pass through too many hands. Use the loop and the extra man with discretion. Create space rather than close it down.

Lineouts

The same choices confront an outside-half at the lineout except that there will

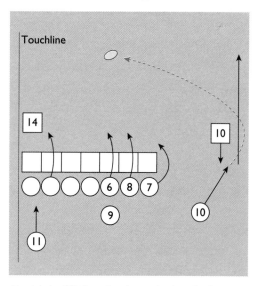

Outside-half kicking back into the box for his forwards after receiving the ball from the line-out.

be no blind-side to exploit. Lineout ball is quicker because the scrum-half simply has to catch and give. It is from lineouts that an outside-half may have fractionally more time to initiate midfield ploys. He will have the whole width of the field to exploit.

Kicking

An outside-half must be a supreme tactical kicker, able to use either foot to punt the ball accurately. If he gets quick service from a lineout, he has the option of kicking back into the box so that his forwards can run on to it. The kick should be high and well-placed and the outside-half must be sure to put his pack on-side.

The long, raking diagonal kick can be used to gain ground and put the defence under pressure. The ball must be put into the space behind the advancing three-quarters and to the side of the full-back so that he has to turn and chase back with the attacking centres and wings on his heels.

The perfect diagonal kick trickles near the corner-flag and gives the attacking wing a good chance of winning the race to the try-line. The best that the defending full-back can do is to bundle the ball into touch or take it over his own line and touch it down, thus conceding a five-metre scrum.

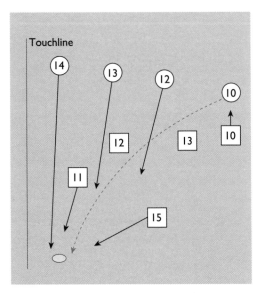

Path of diagonal kick from outside-half, with attacking winger racing the full-back to the ball.

If a three-quarter line comes up quickly in defence, a chip kick over their heads may prove more effective. Outside-half or centres can run through to gather the ball which will drop into the space behind the three-quarters but in front of the full-back.

The up-and-under will always test a defence if it is accurate and used at the right time. Lift the ball high enough to give your centres time to reach the full-back as he catches the ball so they can apply maximum pressure.

Do not over-use any one of these kicks. A judicious mix of all of them is required. There may even be an occasion when you take the opportunity to go down the blind-side of a scrum and put in a cross kick to the centre of the field.

Kicking practice should be part of every training routine because skill with the boot is such an important facet of the outside-half's game.

Drop Kick

This deserves a special mention because it can win matches. Opportunities do not come along often so you must seize them when they do. A scrum under the opposition posts is the classic position for an attempted drop goal because the outside-half can lie deep enough to give himself room and yet be well within his range.

A lineout deep in enemy territory may also deliver the quick ball that the outside-half needs. Or it may come from broken play when a snap goal is the only scoring option. I was a drop-kick specialist and held the British club record for the most drop goals in a season. This did not mean I took a pot-shot at the posts whenever I was within range. In many games, I never had the chance to even try a drop kick. But when a good opportunity did come, I was ready to exploit it and gain a valuable three points for my team.

During practice sessions, work to perfect your drop-outs to the forwards from restarts at the halfway and 22-metre lines. But always find time to rehearse your drop goals as well.

Defence

It is in defence that an outside-half really needs to be a two-footed player. He may be called upon to put the ball into touch under severe pressure and may not have time to get it on to his stronger foot. Accuracy is more important than length with all kicks out of defence. Get it safely into touch at all costs.

Practise with other players as described in the section on full-back play. If no other player is available, use cones to mark the place where you wish the ball to land. Always have a target during kicking practice.

When you kick from outside your 22-metre area, the ball must bounce before it goes into touch. This is a more difficult skill to master. The perfect kick will bounce one metre from the touchline before rolling over it. None of its power will be wasted and it will travel the full distance.

Practise receiving the ball from your scrum-half and kicking to touch as two defenders close in on you. Near the left-hand touchline, you will kick with your right foot and vice versa. Lower the angle if you are kicking into a strong wind so that the ball is not blown off course. If the wind is at your back, use it by giving the ball more height.

Accurate kicking is the easiest way of relieving pressure and getting into the opposing half of the field. But do not let

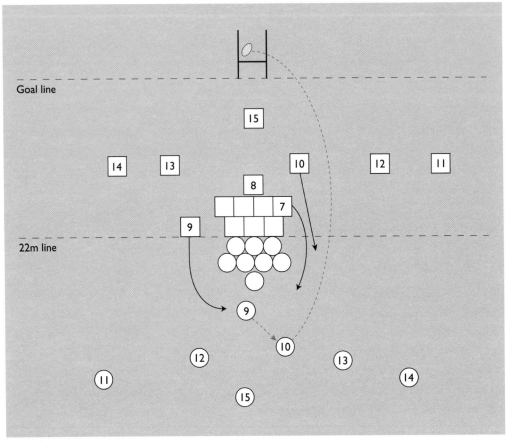

Outside-half positioned for drop goal from scrum on opposition 22-metre line.

kicking dominate your whole game. Rugby must always remain essentially a handling code.

Positioning

This will depend on whether you are employing a man-to-man defence or a drift defence. If it is the former, you will defend in channels and must come up on your opposite number from the set-pieces.

Go up fast on your man to limit his options. This is particularly important at a scrum because you will be closer to him than your flanker and will thus exert the first pressure on him. If he passes, cover behind your centres.

With a drift-defence, you run for the inside-centre and put pressure on him. If he passes the ball, you should again continue on behind your centres to provide cover.

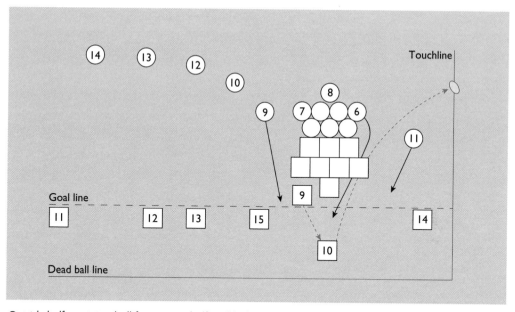

Outside-half receiving ball from scrum-half and kicking to touch as two players converge on him.

Les Cusworth in action against Ireland.

Summary

Great outside-halves are a dying breed. Rugby today does not allow them the time or the space to express themselves. At the top level, they are often no more than a cog in a well-oiled machine. When winning a game is all-important, individual skills must be subdued in favour of team performance.

This is a pity. I was lucky enough to play the game when flair was at a premium and wise coaches encouraged it. Chalkie White implanted the right attitude when he was in charge at Leicester. Throw the ball around.

Open up whenever an opportunity presents itself – even from under your own posts. Attack from a defensive situation and you take the opposition by surprise.

The half-backs are the fulcrum of the team. If they operate smoothly as a unit, you can play fifteen-man rugby. The outside-half must distribute the ball intelligently in attack and fulfil his duties in defence. But he should always look for that chance to do the unexpected, to make that break, to commit himself, to improvise. His position carries immense responsibility with it but he should never lose sight of the sheer fun of being a fly-half.

Back-Row

Nairn MacEwan

The wing-forwards in any team are the essential catalysts in both attack and defence. A team lacking a back-row with the right blend of effectiveness and quality is severely handicapped. It can affect the continuity of play in attack and disrupt vital possession at the breakdown.

Gone are the days when a wing-forward was principally an aggressive intimidator and destroyer. He must now be an all-round rugby athlete.

Individual Qualities

1. He must be a complete all-round athlete with excellent co-ordination and a high level of reflex and reaction.
2. He needs the physical power and stamina to perform the close-quarter work as a forward; and the pace of a back to give support in attack and defence.
3. A high level of fitness is essential and he must have the body strength to secure the ball and remain on his feet under pressure.
4. Split-second assessment and anticipation are required in all phases of the game.
5. He must be a decisive tackler, who is effective against powerful, driving forwards as well as fast, skilful backs.
6. He should possess a secure handling ability along with the basic skills of back play to enable him to support like an extra three-quarter in attack and defence. All wing-forwards should practise with the back-division, even occasionally playing with them to learn their lines of running, their set moves and their general style of play. The back-row must also be well-versed in their defensive patterns and alignment.
7. An instinctive urge to secure or recover possession of the ball is a must.

The ultimate number 8 Wayne Shelford of New Zealand, a commanding presence on any rugby field.

A wing-forward should have a constant awareness of the movement and whereabouts of the ball, matched by an almost shark-like readiness to get to it either as possessor or protector.

8. The ideal wing-forward has character, personality, rugby intelligence and skill, together with the pace and power that Nature bestows on a successful predator. Without these varied talents, nobody can become a legend like Michael Jones of New Zealand or Jean-Pierre Rives of France. The back-row demands extremely high standards.

The Back-Row Unit

Wing-forwards have to possess all the individual qualities listed above. As part of the back-row, however, they have varying roles and must blend together as a closely coordinated and effective unit.

Whether a team opts for a formation of left and right flankers – or open and blind-side – is a matter of choice. It often depends on the abilities of the players available for selection.

Open and Blind-Side Formation

Many teams opt for the fast, wide-ranging, open-side flanker and the more combative blind-side specialist, who usually has more bulk and strength but not the explosive pace of his colleague.

This formation has its merits and the choice usually depends on the talent available and the style of game that the team elects to play.

Left or Right Formation

However, good flankers should be interchangeable. So wing-forwards selected on the left and right of the scrum may well prove to be a more effective combination. There is the added advantage of a consistently higher performance level on the open part of the ground with the flankers alternating between open and blind-side during a game. They achieve a better balance of energy loss, and they avoid the negative effect on the team of injury to a specialist open or blind-side flanker.

By having two flankers of real quality – and scorching pace in covering the ground – a team's performance will gain an enormous benefit in both attack and defence.

The Pivot Five

The back-row has to work in conjunction with the half-backs in every area of the game. Each unit has its functions and their specific roles must be disciplined and harmonious.

The back-row and the half-backs are the pivot on which the whole team revolves.

When the ball is static, the back-row must have it under constant observation. So must the half-backs. Once the ball is released in open play, it triggers off either an attacking ploy or some defensive action.

Immediately the back-row see that the ball is out, they can move. Without this ball-awareness and correctly judged reflex action, the back-row unit will be less effective and may give away costly penalties at the base of the scrum.

Defence at the Scrum

Open-Side

Here is a situation that will occur in every game. There is a scrum near the touch-line. The attacking side has the put-in. Its back-division line up for a move on the open-side. As soon as the ball is out of the scrum, the back-row of the defending team must go into action.

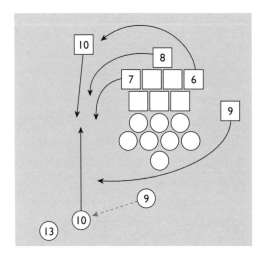

The back-row breaks from the scrum to support their own scrum-half.

The scrum-half (9) pressurises his opposite number. When the ball is released, however, he is the nearest defender to the opposition back-line. He moves towards the outside-half (10) on the inside.

The defending open-side flanker (7) is on the heels of his scrum-half in pursuit of the opposition outside-half. The defending outside-half runs at his opposite number to complete the pincer movement. If the ball is transferred along the line, the defenders follow the movement across the field.

Flankers Peter Winterbottom and Mike Teague are the first to support Will Carling's midfield break.

The defending number 8 and blind-side flanker will run diagonally on a secondary line of defence to cover a break or a kick by the opposition.

If the scrum is on the other side of the field, the same defensive action is followed in reverse. The open-side flanker harries the opposition backs while his back-row colleagues provide the cover.

In a highly organised and efficient team, the outside-half can be utilised in a deeper, defensive role where his pace can provide additional cover. He does not advance on his opposite number because he is confident that his scrum-half and open-side flanker can contain him.

This system not only improves the cover defence, especially in bad weather conditions. It also releases the defending outside-half from primary tackling duties and keeps him free to use his running and handling skills.

Blind Side

Take the same situation of a scrum near the touchline. The attacking team again had the put-in. This time, however, they opt for a blind-side move. In this case, the defending back-row must be fully on

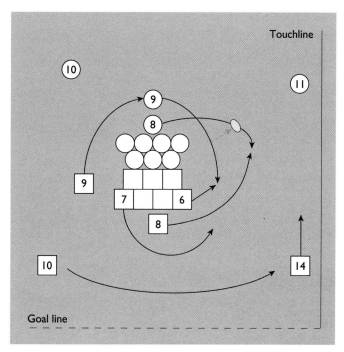

Scrum near the line *The attacking side try a blind-side move. The defending back-row counter it as described below.*

the alert and go swiftly into action.

The defending scrum-half (9) harries his opposite number.

The defending blind-side flanker (6) advances as soon as the ball is out of the scrum and tackles the first attacking player who starts to run with the ball. This may be the scrum-half or the number 8. Ideally, the flanker should tackle his man before the latter reaches the gain line.

The defending number 8 takes the second attacker.

The defending open-side flanker (7) and outside-half (10) will move to the blind-side to cover deeper positions in conjunction with their blind-side winger (14).

Near the try line, room for manoeuvre will be limited. The defending number 8 may not have time to get up from the scrum and take out the second attacker. If his pack is strong enough to hold their own in the scrum, the number 8 may detach himself completely and stand on the blind-side as a more effective defender.

Attack at the Scrum

Back-Row Moves

The back-row can be used as an attacking unit from the base of the scrum. These are well-rehearsed ploys to penetrate the opposition defence and score, especially near the opposition line. If unsuccessful, these ploys still create an opportunity to break the gain line and deliver good second-phase possession.

The ideal configuration is a scrum near the touchline and within striking distance of the opposition goal-line. On their put-in, the attacking side calls a back-row move.

The attacking number 8 picks up the ball and runs up the blind-side to draw the opposition blind-side flanker (6).

The ball is passed to the attacking scrum-half (9) who is running on a wide arc outside his number 8. The scrum-half

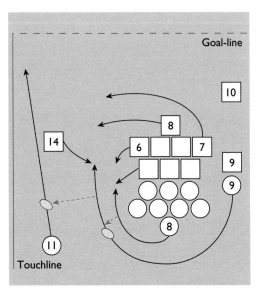

Scrum near the opposition goal line *The attacking side calls the move described below.*

runs towards the defending wing (14) to create a two-to-one situation with his own left-wing (11).

The defending number 8 may be quick and alert enough to cover this danger but the attacking open-side flanker (6) will have come round to the blind-side to run on his inside through an undefended area. The left-wing (11) passes inside for his open-side flanker to score.

If the scrummage is near the opposite touchline, the roles of the attacking players are simply reversed.

Next is a back-row ploy that can be used from a scrum that is almost anywhere on the field. It must be practised time and again so that the movement

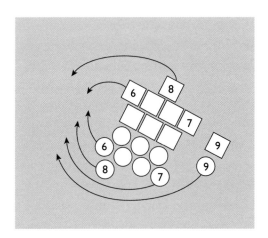

A back-row ploy to be used almost anywhere on the field as described below.

becomes both speedy and fluent.

The attacking number 8 takes up a position between the left-flanker and the left-lock. The ball is directed to the feet of the number 8. The scrum is wheeled slightly in this direction so that the opposition flanker (7) and number 8 are removed from immediate defensive positions.

The attacking number 8 lifts the ball and turns to back into a much-weakened defence.

At the same time, the attacking right-flanker (7) detaches himself from the scrum to loop around. He takes the ball from his number 8 with driving force.

The attacking left-flanker (6) will be at his side to lend further support. Once the initial surge is created, the other forwards in attack can detach and drive in support.

Lineout

Defence

Below are the standard positions taken up by a defending back-row at a lineout where the opposition have the throw-in.

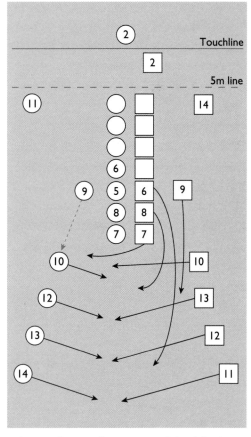

A lineout showing the positions of the defending back-row as described below.

The left-flanker (6), the number 8 and the right flanker (7) are standing in that order at the back of the lineout.

The ball is thrown in and won by the

attacking side. The scrum-half passes it to his outside-half.

The defending right-flanker (7) is closest to the opposition outside-half and will run directly at him.

His number 8 will run on a slightly deeper defensive line that takes him across the pitch.

The defending left-flanker (6) runs on an even deeper defensive line behind his own back-division so that he can cover any break by opposition three-quarters or cope with any kick ahead.

There is an important variation to this standard defence. Lineout ball can be the best ball for an attacking side and hence the most dangerous for the defending team. In certain positions on the field, therefore, it is worth considering this alternative.

The six defending players in the lineout are stretched to cover the seven attacking forwards. The shorter of the two defending flankers is detached and deployed to give extra cover to the back-line.

The two most useful positions for this additional defender (number 6) are as follows:

He can come in between his centre and wing and thereby cover the intrusion of the attacking side's full-back.

Or he can become an auxiliary full-back, well-placed to cover any midfield breaks or to intercept any tactical kicks from attacking players.

Attack

The number 8 may well be used as one of the regular jumpers and may alter his

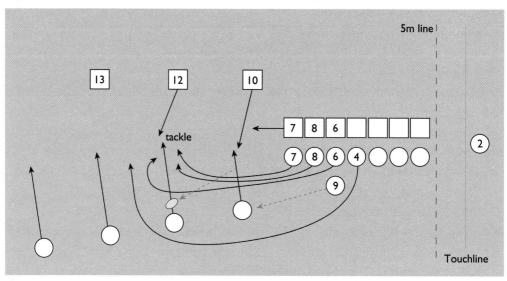

The back row on the attack from a line out when it is their throw-in.

Dominique Erbani of France and Dean Richards of England at the rear of the lineout.

position at the lineout to keep the opposition guessing.

The back-row may also be involved in a long throw that is tapped down by the number 8 to the flanker in front of him who peels around.

Once the ball is secured in a lineout, the back-row must go immediately in support. As the ball is fed along their back division, they must run hard to get to any breakdown before their opposite numbers and to retain possession. It is vital to keep the momentum going. The back-row has a key role in continuity of play.

When they are in attack – at lineout, scrum or breakdown – the back-row must know the intended point of penetration through the defence so that they can give the correct line of support. They must think quicker and move faster than their opposite numbers.

Summary

The back-row are vital to the overall performance of a team. While they can have moments of individual brilliance, each player must clearly understand his specific role and work in harmony with his two colleagues as part of the pivot-five.

Wing-forwards are given opportunities for glory that are usually denied the front-five but they must earn those opportunities. They are involved in every phase of the game and must bring total commitment to the task in hand.

Given the excessive demands made on today's back-row, it is not surprising that they sometimes fall short of perfection. Great back-row forwards are indeed born and not made.

□ □

Second-Row

....➤

Peter Brown

I was first introduced to rugby football in 1955 when I was only thirteen. Despite all the changes that have taken place in the Laws, spirit and appeal of the game, one decisive fact remains – successful and enjoyable rugby stems from the necessity of winning regular, controlled set-piece ball, be it from scrummage, lineout or kick-off.

The most important single providers of such possession are the two second-rows. They will be the two tallest men on the field, bulky athletes, endowed with natural spring and with well-developed upper leg and body strength. Good hand-eye co-ordination allied to natural spring is the raw material. Bodily strength and scrummaging ability can be acquired.

The ideal second-row is a committed, brave, ambitious 6'5" ball-playing athlete. It has long been argued that the ideal second-row combination at international level is a 6'6"/7" seventeen-stone middle-of-the-line jumper with a 6'4" eighteen-stone front-line jumper – someone like brother Gordon at the height of his powers when he toured with the Lions in South Africa in 1974. These big men need an immense amount of physical training to develop the muscle bulk and time required to hold a scrum rock steady on their own put-in. They must also be alert and sharp enough to accomplish a 21–23-inch standing jump to win lineout balls from the first to the eightieth minute of an all-out game. The second-row forward never gets any chance to relax or gather his breath during a game.

My optimum combination, in fact, would be two 6'5" sixteen to sixteen-and-a-half-stone second-rows, natural athletes who can support each other, and jump at any position in the lineout. One player would be right-handed, the other left.

Scrum

Many hours of playing and practice are required. It is necessary to acquire the mirror skills needed to scrummage equally well on both the left and right-hand side of the second-row. It has to become second nature (automatic pilot, in fact) to reach the point of scrummage and go through the familiar routine:

(i) Put your arm round your fellow second-row and grasp the top of his shorts.

(ii) Crouch down.

(iii) Insert your other arm fully through to the shoulder between the legs of the prop in front of you and curl it round to grip the thigh of his inner leg.

(iv) Take the strain.

The main power and apex of the scrum is formed from the two second-rows' outside shoulders through the inner thighs of the props. The cementing bond is the interlocking of the inside arms of the two second-rows.

Within this framework, the hooker operates. His position in the scrum dictates the positions of the second-rows' heads. When preparing to receive his own scrummage feed or put-in, the

The front-five in scrummaging mode.

hooker will sit as far as possible to his left on the right shoulder of the left-hand second-row. The latter's great problem is what to do with his own head because, if the second-row had no head, the hooker would get that bit further across to the incoming ball!

It is much rarer these days, on the opposition put-in, for the hooker to sit across to his right to attempt to hook the ball against the head. It is much more often the case that he brings both legs back into the middle of the scrum so that, together with the props and the second-row, he forms a solid attacking base from which his pack can mount an eight-man shove or a controlled wheel. Changes in the law have limited the extent and effectiveness of the wheel but the well-timed shove is still an excellent way to deprive the opposition of its own ball at a scrummage.

A definite fault in modern scrummaging technique occurs when the left-hand second-row, on receipt of his own ball, is not fully committed to the shove. The problem is that his position in the scrum is awkward because of the hooker sitting across preparatory to striking the ball; and the second-row is keen to play his part in channelling the ball to the feet of the number 8.

So often have I watched teams scrummage powerfully and menacingly on the opposition put-in, and yet seem equally vulnerable on their own put-in. This is due to the modern obsession for the back-row pick up and drive from a wheeling scrum, often supported by the second-row from the side opposite the intended peel-off.

In my view, scrummaging in this way makes a team vulnerable to a well-timed, concentrated eight-man shove. The solution is for the left-hand second-row of the team with the put-in to adjust his position so that he is able to give a 100 per cent shove to help to hold the opposition drive.

Left and Right

A second-row must be able to play equally well on either side of the scrum. All my early years were spent on the left side and it wasn't until I took part in the Scottish Trial in 1965 that I was forced to play on the right. Peter Stagg was my partner and he, too, was a left-sided second-row. In the new position, I felt highly insecure and was unable to concentrate. The next season, I played right-hand second-row for West of Scotland so that I became equally conversant with both positions.

Hookers

Hookers can be dangerous. When the scrum is set for an eight-man shove, the pressure on the opposition hooker is intense because he is expected to win his own ball. The greedy and ambitious hooker will change his body position at the last second to be able to strike against the head. So tightly has the scrummage been bound that the abrasive movement of his shorts can scrape the flesh off the cheek bones of a tightly packed second-row. I have sternly warned my own hooker for persistently doing this. Reason with him first. And work out a compromise on the practice field.

Preparation

This is most important. Boot studs must at all times be 100 per cent. The maximum stress occurs in a scrummage close to your own line when the opposition have the put-in.

The second-rows have to put their feet right back, put as many studs as possible in the ground and dig in deep to lock in their legs. They must provide stability and prevent the scrummage from moving. The attacking team will often attempt a pushover try in the first instance. A second option may well be a back-row move. In this case, the defending blind-side wing-forward will detach, leaving the other seven members of his pack to withstand the shove. This will put even greater stress on the defending second-rows.

Weight and size are not everything. In the days before boot inspections, Alistair McHarg and I wore the longer heel studs in our soles. We did not possess the weight and bulk of normal international second-rows – but neither Al nor I were ever normal. We were outstanding athletes with powerful frames which we could use to optimum advantage. John Reason, the rugby writer, once criticised the Barbarians for playing a powder-puff

Scrummaging position of second-rows.

second-row and predicted that we would be taken apart by the Tigers in the annual Baa Baas game at Leicester. Al and I made him eat his words when we scored a pushover try against their much-vaunted scrummaging pack. If you know how to time and concentrate your shove, you will be able to disrupt heavier packs.

Regardless of the advantage you may have in a scrum, it is no place to rest. Once the solid platform has been supplied, the second-rows must disengage immediately and sprint in the direction of the next potential breakdown.

This requires great fitness and speed of thought. You must develop the ball-awareness that all good players have. Build up your strength for scrummaging

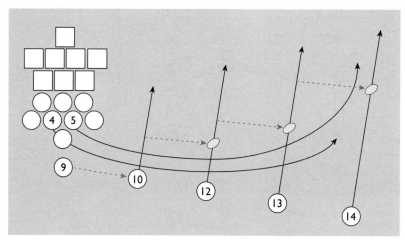

Second-row at the break-up of a scrummage.

and always practise with your front-row. You will need powerful biceps for binding and for mauling. Work on improving your speed about the pitch and the effectiveness of your tackling.

The psychological advantage of a good scrum is enormous. A team which can rely on a steady supply of good ball on its own put-in will be full of confidence. The second-rows are there to generate the

power needed in a good scrum and to mastermind the disruption of the opposition on their ball.

Lineouts

For many years, I gained selection at top level because of my spring and dexterity at the lineout. My ambition was such that I wanted the ball to be thrown at me every time. But I was a good enough team member to recognise that the best option is where the two main second-row lineout jumpers and the number 8 liaise in supporting each other. This gives the thrower three possible targets and creates variation.

Second-rows should also utilise the ball-gathering skills of props like David Sole who had cricket catch-taking hands. Props are particularly useful at the lineout because of their low centre of gravity. If the ball can be deflected or dropped down into their waiting hands, they are ideally placed to drive through the gaps in the lineout to create very good second-phase ball.

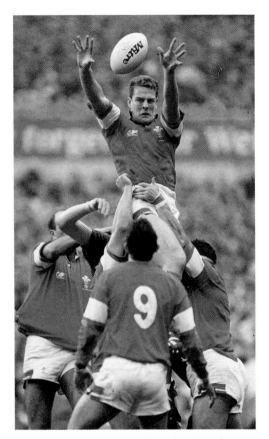

Spring-heeled Gareth Llewellyn of Wales wins another lineout.

Winning lineout ball is all to do with practice and ambition. In good weather conditions, a lineout expert who is matched against an equally accomplished jumper, should, on his own throw-in, always get the first hand or finger-tip to the ball. The jumper's options vary. He can:

(i) Jump straight up and catch the ball two-handed.

(ii) Jump forward and catch the ball two-handed.

(iii) Jump back and catch the ball two-handed.

(iv) Go even higher in all three positions and pull the ball down one-handed.

For maximum efficiency, he will deflect the ball either from in front or behind. The best possible lineout ball an outside centre can receive is first-time

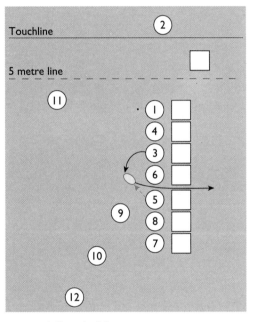

Jumper deflects ball for prop 3.

deflected ball from the lineout expert standing at four or five. The ball is directed to the outside shoulder of the scrum-half who passes immediately to the outside-half. He, in turn, throws out a pass which misses out the inside-centre and goes straight to his midfield partner. The outside-centre is now into his stride with the ball in his arms without any danger of his marker – some twenty metres away – getting near him.

It takes a lot of practice but it is lethally effective. In 1964, before the days of backs lying ten metres back at the lineout, I was asked to deflect the ball down to the outside hand of Eck Hastie at scrum-half so that he got it as early as possible. He

metres from the lineout, an attacking side will create even more space with this type of lineout ball.

Technique

It is essential for the successful jumper to get his shoulder or hand in first when going forward; and to delay his jump and play the ball at the apex of that jump when going back.

When you are the designated jumper

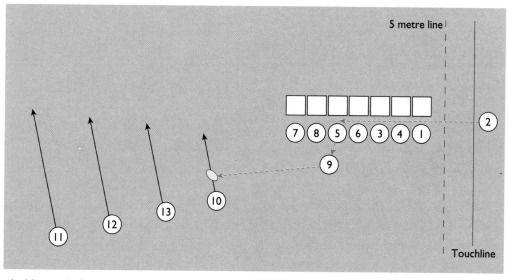

Ideal lineout ball.

then fed his outside-half, Davy Chisholm, who could either use a miss move to get the ball to his outside-centre or side-step inside the marauding wing-forwards. This ploy served Scotland well, especially against the touring Australians in 1965 when Chisholm scored a try from it. With the opposing three-quarters standing ten

at a lineout, your thrower must know which type of jump you will use to take the ball so that he can put it in exactly the right place.

Practice, practice, practice. It is particularly vital in view of all the bumping contact with your opposite number before you get in the air. You have to be robust enough to absorb a bump yet still get maximum height on your jump.

131

Defending lineout *Lineout for defending side near their goal-line. Second-row stands at front to force longer throw.*

The contact between the packs in the first lineout of the 1991 World Cup semi-final between England and Scotland was over-aggressive. If the Scottish pack had all squatted down on a pre-arranged signal, the seven marking Englishmen would have ended up on their noses as they barged across. England were determined to make their weight advantage tell in every way.

The first hand to the ball so often wins it. When I stood at number four in the line, with my right shoulder towards the opposition goal-line, I was able to play the ball much higher with my right hand. Jumping with my left shoulder towards the opposition goal-line, I used my left hand to push away my opponent so that I could go over the top to play the ball with my right. (The experimental law introduced for the 1992–93 season would have outlawed this second play as it stipulated that only the jumper's inside hand could be used to play the ball.) When I was jumping at the front of the lineout, I invariably tried to catch the ball.

Positioning

This is crucial. On the opposition throw-in close to their own line, it is imperative to place your best jumper at number one, standing on the 5-metre line. This prevents the much-favoured fast, hard throw to the stomach of an early jumper. The defending thrower is forced to throw the ball deeper into the line and thereby increase the danger of having it pirated by the attacking team.

Do not hold up your inside arm as the hooker is about to throw. It does not distract him and it presents a very inviting, unprotected under-arm and rib area for the shoulder of the opposing prop. Holding an arm up also impedes your own jump. The throwing up of both arms in the air increases the height of your leap and your chances of interception.

On your own throw-in, give yourself

room to jump. Keep your opposite number guessing until the ball is in the air. Beat him with the speed, height and angle of your jump.

A taller man will not necessarily out-jump you. I have been very impressed in recent times by the activity, mobility and subterfuge of the Japanese second-row. They counter-act their lack of height by shuffling positions in the line and changing the body angle of their jump. They work extremely well in concert with their props. Early in 1992, the new Scottish second-row also demonstrated how effective you can be by changing your body position at the last moment in order to capitalise on the fact that you know exactly where the ball will be thrown.

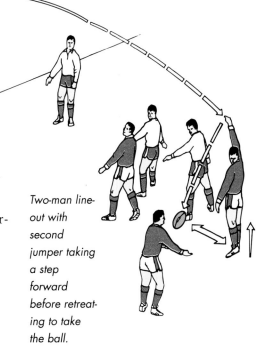

Two-man line-out with second jumper taking a step forward before retreat-ing to take the ball.

Short Lineouts

The mobile and dextrous second-row should win the ball on every occasion on his own throw. He knows whether to go backwards or forwards to it and that should be sufficient, if the throw is accu-rate, to lose his marker. He can further confuse his opponent with a feint and clean up.

Brother Gordon and I worked most effectively together off short lineouts for our country because we were on the same wavelength as our thrower. Constant practice was our secret. We perfected this area of our game and the opposition never stood a chance.

If it is an opposition throw, do every-thing to impede and pressurise their two jumpers. They have the advantage but you must be quick-witted enough to weaken it. Remember that it is easier to go forward than back. If you stand slightly behind your opposite number, you can keep him fully in your sights. Put him under enough pressure and the mistakes are bound to come.

Front-Row

Sandy Carmichael

The front-row is the foundation of the pack. Each player must be a specialist in his position but they must operate as an effective unit. Winning a game starts in the front-row. If they cannot impose themselves on the opposition and secure good ball, there will be no solid forward platform.

A front-row is no place for the faint-hearted. You will need strength, skill, speed, tenacity and experience. It takes time to mature and achieve full potential in the front-row. My long international career allowed me to play with or against outstanding performers like Fran Cotton, John Pullin, Peter Wheeler, Ian McLauchlan, Ray McLoughlin, Ken Kennedy, Sean Lynch and the famous Pontypool front-row of Graham Price, Charlie Faulkner and Bobby Windsor. These British stalwarts were feared and respected throughout world rugby. And they were durable players. Props and hookers can certainly stand the pace.

The high standards have continued on down into the 1990s with such great competitors as David Sole, Richard Loe, Phil Kearns, Jeff Probyn, Ewen McKenzie and Sean Fitzpatrick. The Irish front-row of Nick Popplewell, Keith Wood and Peter Clohessy is a strong combination and the English trio of Jason Leonard, Brian Moore and Victor Ubogo offer a wonderful blend of power, skill and experience. The pace of today's game means that they have to be fine all-round athletes who thrive on action. The front-row is a combat zone.

Scrum

It all begins here. Scrummaging technique wins or loses games. The front-row plays a decisive role. They must always go down as a unit, support each other, know when and how to shove. They

Eight-man scrummage forming.

must also have a good understanding with the rest of their forwards. A well-drilled pack that has learned how to concentrate its power can often push a heavier set of forwards off the ball. It comes down to skill and timing.

Go down low and keep your back straight. Anchor the legs so they can take the strain and allow you to shove hard.

The front-row must transmit the power of the five men behind them. If the props push at the wrong angle, the force of the shove is displaced and they lose control.

An experienced front-row will know how to use every ounce of power in their pack to the best advantage. They will angle their shove correctly and bore into

the opposition front-row to good effect.

To achieve this kind of unity, you must practise regularly. The best way to do this is against another pack of forwards of equivalent weight and power. If this is not possible, a valuable alternative is the scrummaging machine. It is a piece of equipment that pays good dividends for any club. Scrummaging machines are much more sophisticated than they used to be. You can not only practise your scrummaging technique endlessly against rock-solid opposition, you can also develop the strength of your neck, back and legs.

The front-row unit consists of three specialists. The loose-head prop, the hooker and the tight-head prop must not just master their own positions. Each must appreciate the needs and skills of his two colleagues. Props will always have a preference but they must be able to play in either position in an emergency. Versatility will increase their changes of being selected.

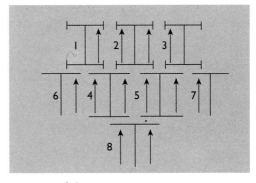

Direction of shove in scrummage.

Loose-Head Prop

The loose-head prop is so-called because he packs down on the left-hand side of the front-row with his head outside that of his opposite number. This is the more difficult position of the two. He must stabilise the scrum for the hooker and make sure that the latter can see the ball as it comes in. The best way to do this is to get as low as possible without collapsing the scrum. This requires strength and timing. As he goes into a scrum, the loose-head prop will put his head under the chest of the opposition tight-head. Use a wide leg-base to get support. Keep your inside foot back so that it does not impede the passage of the ball when it his hooked.

Make sure that your second-row is providing a secure base as you hit the opposition front-row. Your flanker must also be locked in behind you. After your initial crouch, take one step in and engage. The scrum is now formed.

If it is your ball, you will put your feet farther back to take the strain and absorb the drive of the opposition. If it is their ball, adjust your feet so that you can shove hard when the ball comes in. Disrupt the opposition by applying pressure slowly and steadily, and by changing the angle of your drive. Aggression is important but do not make quick hostile movements in the front-row. They only provoke. If you build up your endurance,

you will be able to put your opposite number under pressure in every scrum.

Binding is critical. The hooker will bind over the shoulders of both props and get a firm hold on their shirts under the armpits. The loose-head prop will lock his right arm around the hooker's body and find a secure grip on his shirt. Do not hinder the lateral movement of the hooker's hips. He may need to swing to strike at the ball. Use your left hand to grip your opposite number's arm.

Collapsing a scrum is illegal and dangerous. It serves no point. Lifting your opposite number will also be penalised. The strength and angle of your shove are the most potent weapons. Practise these by one-to-one scrummag-

Binding in the front row.

ing sessions on the training ground to build up your power and speed of response. Scrummage against a variety of partners so that you learn to adapt to each opponent's build and technique.

Tight-Head Prop

The tight-head prop is so called because his head is locked tight in every scrum between that of the opposing hooker and loose-head. His main role is to protect his own hooker. On his own ball, he must provide stability and counter the drive from the other pack. This is best done by packing low with feet well-spaced for anchorage.

Good binding is again vital. The tight-head must lock his arm across the back of his hooker and grip his shirt. The loose-head prop will bind on to the hooker first but the tight-head will engage fractionally sooner as the front-rows meet. It is important that he gets his neck and shoulders in the correct position to enable him to maximise his power. He can lessen the effectiveness of his opponents by changing the angle of his shove. Though he is locked in the heart of the scrum, he is still able to make telling adjustments.

The loose-head prop has to be immensely strong because he gets the whole weight of the opposition tight-head bearing down on him plus the forward drive of the other pack. The tight-head, by contrast, will get more weight coming on him from a horizontal direction. He is able to pack slightly lower to absorb this because he does not have to worry about keeping the scrum up to let the ball in.

Like all members of the front-row, the tight-head prop must be streetwise. Even the most vigilant referees cannot see everything that goes on in the scrum. Props and hookers must learn to look after themselves and earn the respect of the opposition front-rows. Never descend to dirty play. A good tight-head prop can wear down and destroy the loose-head in the opposition front-row and severely handicap the hooker.

Hooker

The hooker is in the most vulnerable position of all. His name denotes his duty in the scrum. He must hook his own ball every time and try to get as many strikes against the head on the opposition put-in. Hookers need strength, speed and great agility. The skill factor is crucial.

Bind over the shoulders of your props and get a firm grip on their shirts under the armpits. They will lock their arms across your back so that the front-row is a solid unit. When you engage with the opposition scrum, you will have the force of a seven-man shove to support you and give you the freedom to strike for the ball when it comes in.

Hooking must be practised constantly with your scrum-half. The front-row may practice the basic movements with the aid of a scrummage machine. Timing and accuracy can be improved this way as can the relationship with your scrum-half. But a three-on-three situation is more valuable because it forces you to make the kinds of adjustments you will need to make in a match.

Speedy ball from a scrum gives the back-line a distinct advantage. Every hooker must therefore be able to deliver quick-channel ball. Before the scrum goes down, the hooker knows what kind of heel has been called. He should keep very close to his loose-head so that he is near to the ball as he can be when his scrum-half puts it in. The opposition tight-head prop will bore in to try to affect his vision of the ball but his own loose-head prop should counter this.

As the ball comes in, one swift strike is all that is needed. The ball is clipped away with the sole of the foot through the tunnel behind him and straight out to the scrum-half.

If a slower ball is needed so that it can be held in the pack, then the hooker will use a different technique. As the ball comes in from his scrum-half, he is in the same strike position but will use his heel more and sweep the ball back. The ball is literally hooked and protected

Bound for business: French front-rows are tough and uncompromising.

more. It can be controlled by the number 8 for a pushover try or to initiate a back-row ploy.

There is a third variation used by some teams. The hooker delivers slow-channel ball at a different angle so that it goes to the right of the number 8, enabling him to pick it straight up and begin a movement. All three methods need careful rehearsal. The hooker has no margin for error.

On the opposition put-in, the hooker must time his strike perfectly in order to offset the advantage that his opposite number has in being closer to the ball. If the loose-head prop can disrupt the opposing hooker, his own might be able

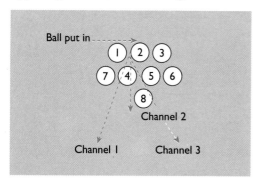

Channelling the ball in scrummage.

to take the ball against the head with a perfectly timed strike. It is very demoral-ising for any hooker and for his team to forfeit such a ball. Always go for the strike against the head. Make your oppo-nent fight for every ball that his scrum-half puts in.

A front-row must work in harmony with its scrum-half. He will put the ball into the scrum in the way that the hooker prefers. When the ball has been hooked – or lost – he will also act as the eyes of the whole pack. Locked into their positions, the front-row in particular will need to be told where the ball is and when it leaves the scrum.

Lineout

Hooker

After the physical struggle of the scrum, the hooker takes on a precision job at the lineout. He throws the ball in. It is a diffi-cult skill but it must be mastered as there will be several lineouts in a normal game. At a seven-man lineout, he will usually have three options. He can throw the ball to the first jumper near the front of the line; to the second jumper near the middle; or to the third jumper at the tail.

A fourth possibility is the long throw which clears the lineout completely and lands in open ground for the centres to run on to.

All of these throws demand timing and accuracy. The long throw, in particu-lar, needs careful practice and should only be used with discretion. At each lineout, everyone on your side must know where the ball is going. The scrum-half's signal must be clear. The hooker will then know to whom the ball is to be thrown and how that jumper likes to take it.

Regular practice with the jumpers is a must. The ball must be thrown to them with pin-point accuracy so that they can take it cleanly with two hands or deflect it down with one.

Each hooker must follow a routine.

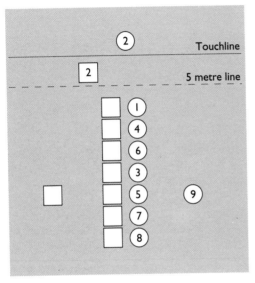

Positions of front-row at lineout.

Do the same thing before every throw. Your right foot should be just behind the touchline and level with the gap between the forwards. Set the ball. Throw it with a smooth action. Use your fingers to get rotation on the ball.

A simple way to improve your accuracy is to practise on the goal-line near the posts. Set yourself a target on the post itself and try to hit it consistently from five metres, then six, then seven and so on.

This will teach you to throw it straight and true but there is no substitute for practice with jumpers. Timing is the key element here. The throw must be gauged to the jumper so that he is taking it at his maximum leap.

Special attention must be paid to the short lineout which may be called by way of a variation. With only two or three men in the line, the hooker must be very careful that his throw does not go adrift.

After the throw, the hooker will cover the blind side and offer support if the scrum-half attempts a break around the front of the lineout.

On the opposition throw-in, the hooker has an attacking role. He polices the blind-side area and must be through on any mistakes. A good hooker will time his run so that he arrives in time to snap up any badly tapped ball. If a scrum-half tries to make a blind-side break, the hooker must take him.

The hooker must be the master of the five-metre area at the front of the line-out. He must control his space forcefully.

Props

The props have a supportive role at the lineouts. They act as minders for the jumpers. One prop will stand at the front of the lineout, as close to the 5-metre line as he can. The other prop will be in the middle of the line.

Each prop will be next to a jumper

and thus able to offer immediate physical support. The other prop will get to the ball as quickly as possible to lend additional support and prevent the opposition forwards from coming through on to the scrum-half. The upper-body strength of the prop makes him an ideal ripper of the ball.

If there is a long throw to the back of the line, the props will peel round to offer support. Props may occasionally catch a deflected or mishandled ball at a lineout but their principal task will always be to support the jumper from behind, to get to the ball quickly, to assist in a drive or to clean up. They will help to stabilise a lineout.

Restarts and Open Play

It is not only in the set-pieces that front-rows make an important contribution. They feature at restarts and in open play. They must develop their running, passing, tackling and kicking skills. Most of the passing will be short and under intense pressure so they must work on close-handling skills.

At kick-offs and restarts, the front-row must be mobile and aggressive. If it is their ball, and the kick is angled towards their touchline, they must pursue it hard and tackle the catcher. For an opposition kick, the props must support their second-rows who are the

Jack the Ripper: Richard Loe, the All Black prop, rips the ball clear before passing back.

most likely catchers. The loose-head prop will support the left-lock and the tight-head will support the right, offering them instant physical cover when they take a ball from the kick-off.

Props are powerhouse players. They will often be used at tap-penalties to bore a hole through the first line of defence before releasing the ball to set up a second-phase attack. A low, driving

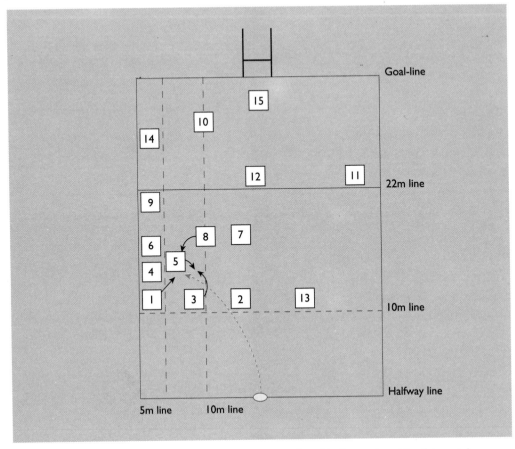

If the second-rows (4) or (5) catch the ball, the props (1) and (3) block on either side of the catcher. Number 8 secures possession from maul.

run will be needed to batter a way through defenders. Knees should have a high, pumping action to generate maximum power.

In open play, the front-row must get to the breakdown quickly and offer support. They must be sound tacklers and natural ball-gatherers. Quickness of thought is a priceless asset. Props and hookers must learn to react with speed to every situation. Then they will have an excellent all-round game.

Front-row forwards are not merely labourers who toil at the rock face of the game. They are specialists with a whole range of skills. In the modern game – with its greater mobility and emphasis on fifteen-man rugby – they are also given more opportunities to get on the scoresheet.

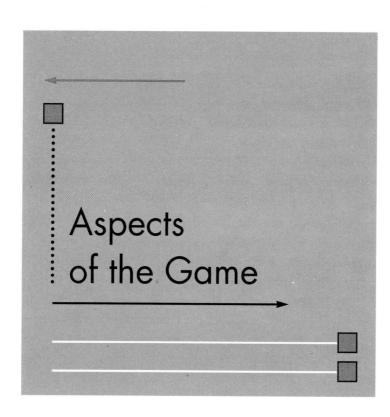

Aspects
of the Game

The Captain

Nairn MacEwan

Selection of the captain for any team is of vital importance. All too often, not enough thought is given to appointing a captain, selection being made on the basis of the best player, the most dominant character, or the most effective motivator. This shows a lack of knowledge or appreciation of the captain's role in modern rugby. It ignores the qualities necessary and underestimates the crucial effect that good leadership can have on the performance of the team.

If the captain lacks the ability to absorb and implement tactical and technical information during the game, it can nullify the potential of a good team as well as the expertise of its coach.

The Captain's Role

Scope and Authority. This centres around the preparation and playing of the game. It is essential that the captain is able to concentrate his time on his responsibilities to the team, and not be burdened with general committee meetings, fund-raising activities and other administrative duties. These were the traditional handicaps from an era when much less commitment was required by players and when there was a lower standard of team preparation than that necessary in the modern game.

The Captain and Coach. The coach should have greater experience, technical expertise, tactical awareness and overall knowledge than the captain. It is the coach who must have complete charge of the organisation and preparation of the team.

However, two-way communication is vital. The captain must be able to contribute his own ideas and those of individual team members. He must monitor the team's reaction and express clearly any difficulties there may be in achieving the coach's aims. This will lead to a unified approach that comes from harmony between captain and coach.

To this end, the captain and coach must give each other mutual respect and loyalty, and be on the same wavelength. The captain can then implement with conviction and clarity the agreed programme, strategy and style.

A good coach will encourage the captain to exercise and establish his leadership and authority during practice, improving his ability as a captain, and becoming completely familiar with the coach's ideas for the team.

As a general rule, during the final practice before a game, the coach should allow the team to play together under the control and guidance of the captain. The coach merely directs a conditioned or unopposed game, confronting the team and its captain with decisions and game situations. This allows the captain to assert his authority, and to test and improve his leadership skills.

It also allows a team to operate as they will in a match.

A wise coach will never overshadow the captain, realising that he cannot allow the team to be reliant on his constant guidance. His object must be to create a team under the direction of the captain that can function efficiently and take correct decisions on its own.

The Match. Once the game starts, the captain is in total control, using his knowledge, leadership and tactical judgement to take his side to victory. An agitated coach who shouts from the sidelines is signalling his own failure to choose and work with the right captain. By yelling advice at the team, he shows an insensitive disregard for the captain's authority and will only create confusion.

While there may be a general game plan, a captain has to have the vision and capacity to change tactics, if necessary, as the match develops. At the same time, he must ensure that the team does not lose its ability to exploit opportunities that occur naturally during a game. He must work hard to retain the right balance, to promote disciplined play that yet leaves room for individual flair and unpredictability.

The captain must instil a sense of discipline in the team, and a respect for the referee and his decisions. He must defuse any heated situations that occur. There will be crucial periods in every game when he will need to put resolution into flagging players or to calm them down in moments of intense pressure. Whenever there is confusion or doubt, the captain must be on hand with direction and encouragement. He must lead and be *seen* to lead.

Motivation. The captain and coach give

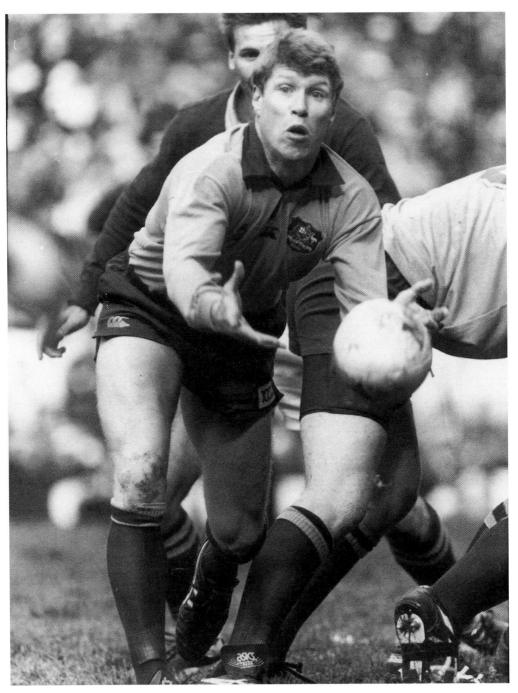

Nick Farr-Jones, captain of Australia: the hands which held the 1991 World Cup.

direction and unity of purpose to the team. This must be supported by motivation to generate a high level of commitment and will to win. This can be developed prior to the game and maintained throughout. The captain is thus the principal motivator.

It is essential that the motivation is not solely channelled towards blind aggression. The team needs a degree of mental and emotional stimulation to achieve the right level of commitment and confidence. However, if it is overdone, it can seriously affect the poise and concentration of players. It can weaken their ability to think and perform as a team.

The individual and collective stimulation must be used to confront the pressure and the task ahead. It must reduce nervous tension to a level where players can still think clearly and perform with confidence.

Players who charge around the changing-room and bang their heads against walls while screaming the numbers one to ten in unison, do not help their team. In trying to psyche themselves up in this attention-seeking way, they disrupt the mental preparation of their colleagues.

Rugby players are not like Kamikaze pilots in the last war who needed to forget that they were on a one-way ticket. A team is there to play thinking rugby. Head-bangers have no place in the game. Controlled aggression allied to playing skills will be vastly more useful on a rugby pitch than those who hurl themselves about with suicidal abandon.

Selection. The captain must have an input in team selection. He will thus be aware of the reasoning behind the choice of certain players and the omission of others. In conjunction with the coach, he can then help to maintain the unity and spirit of the team by giving individuals a precise explanation of why they have been left out. Captain and coach can also advise players in a constructive way how best to improve their performance and chance of selection.

It is important that players understand the decisions of the selectors. They must also have the opportunity to explain their loss of form or touch on other factors that may be relevant. At the same time, players must realise that the final decision rests with the coach and not with the captain. The latter can thus more easily maintain his bond with his team and fulfil his role as a mediator between players, coach and selectors.

Team selection will always be a controversial area because it is impossible to satisfy everyone. Though they try to be fair-minded as they pick what they consider to be the best team available for a particular match, the selectors will sometimes make mistakes. The captain and coach must school the players to accept the decisions taken. Those who may feel they have been unjustly dropped can stake their claim most effectively on the field of play in one of the lower teams. Bickering about selection must be avoided at all costs.

Off the Field. The captain has to take the time to socialise with the opposition after a game and, equally, with his own players. In this way, he can become aware of any personal problems that hinder a player's performance. By helping team-mates at difficult times, he can earn their respect. Winning the trust and loyalty of his colleagues is the essence of successful captaincy.

By taking a genuine interest in his players, by sharing the good times as well as the bad, the captain can create the right spirit and atmosphere off the field. This will be reflected in the team's performance.

A good team spirit is essential in rugby. Without it, the chances of success are very limited. There is immense pressure and commitment in modern rugby, and this must be offset by friendship and shared enjoyment. The captain must understand this and strive to keep the team spirit at the right level in order to produce the attitude, discipline and concentration that he justifiably demands from his players.

Summary. A captain must therefore have qualities of leadership and personality which are just as important as his ability as a player.

He has to enjoy the challenge and responsibility of captaincy. He must never see his position in terms of power and superiority. A captain must serve his team and still be part of it. Nothing can be achieved without the respect and loyalty of his team. He must never compromise these or take them for granted.

A captain has to lead by example and never demand of his team – on or off the field – something which he is not prepared to do himself. Vice-captains must have similar qualities so that they can take over if their skipper is injured during a game and has to leave the field. The new chain of command must preserve continuity.

The great captains of rugby understood their role and felt it a privilege to be given such responsibility. With their character, integrity, commitment, confidence, intelligence and that indefinable touch of charisma, they led their teams to triumphs that would have been impossible without their inspirational leadership.

Coaching

Coaching is an imperative at every level of the game. Major clubs now have full-time professional coaches and some even retain a coaching team to work on specialist areas. At the other end of the sport – with the beginners – coaching is equally important. The way that players are introduced to rugby will have a profound effect on their enjoyment and mastery of the game. Coaches of school teams and Colts sides must therefore be able to communicate an enthusiasm for rugby as well as to cultivate technical expertise.

What makes a good coach? First and foremost, he must command the respect of the players. Without that, he is doomed. If he has the loyalty of his players, he can begin to shape and improve the team in a whole variety of ways. Great coaches have the automatic respect of their players. Carwyn James and Chalkie White were two prime examples.

Their teams trusted them implicitly. The same can be said for such outstanding

Ian McGeechan: a tactical genius for Scotland and the British Lions.

coaches as Bob Dwyer, Roger Uttley, Ian McGeechan, Lawrie Mains, Pierre Berbizier and Jack Rowell. Players will die for such men.

Styles differ enormously. Some coaches never raise their voices while others constantly assault the eardrums. But there are certain qualities that all good coaches need.

Knowledge of the Game

This is fundamental and can only come from playing the game. Coaches need a rugby brain. They must know every aspect of the game and make sure that their teams play it in the right spirit. They must also be able to adapt quickly to changes in the law so that they can coach their players to gain maximum advantage from them.

Leadership

A coach must be a natural leader and motivator. An ability to teach the game is not enough. A coach must be able to put fire into his players and send them out on the pitch in the right frame of mind. Implanting the will to win is crucial. It is easier to lead a successful team. The true test of a coach comes when his team loses matches. He has to pick them up off the floor, make them believe in themselves again and work to eliminate the faults in their game which led to their defeats.

Commitment

A coach cannot expect commitment from the players unless he shows it himself. He must lead by example. Coaching sessions must take priority over everything else. He must always be punctual and well-prepared. Players will take their cue from his attitude so his commitment must be total.

Ambition

Drive and ambition are essentials in a coach. He must strive for success and seek to improve performance. There is no room for compromise or settling for less. An ambitious coach will have the emotional and physical drive necessary to take his team towards the top.

Self-Confidence

This is the bedrock attribute of any coach. He must have the self-confidence to handle his team in the way that he feels is most beneficial to them. Confidence is infectious and will spread throughout the team. Doubts and reservations must be sorted out before he deals with the players. What they must see is a coach with total conviction.

Responsibility

A coach must be ready to accept responsibility for his actions. If he makes mistakes, he must be ready to admit it and make the necessary adjustments. Coaches who enjoy the praises of the victor must also take their share of the responsibility for defeat. They are also answerable for the behaviour of their players on the field. If a team indulges in violence and continued foul play, this is a reflection on their coach as well as on themselves.

Control

No rugby match goes exactly according to plan. There are bound to be setbacks, disappointments and frustrations. A coach who loses control in the face of these things is a poor advertisement for the game. He must have the mental toughness to ride out the stresses and strains. Coaches who abuse a bad referee from the touchline do no favours to their players. They set a bad example of lost discipline.

Determination

Willingness to persevere is another key quality. This is more than commitment to the job in hand. Coaches must have the kind of determination which inspires others to follow. No matter how great the setbacks, they must address their work with unwavering tenacity. This calls for immense emotional and physical stamina.

Adaptability

Good coaches are pragmatic. They adapt quickly to a new set of conditions. As a consequence, their teams become more versatile. A coach should be able to adapt his game plan to neutralise the strengths of the opposition and to make best use of the playing conditions. A coach with a fixed idea of how every game should be played imposes limitations on his players. His team should be able to adopt the style of play most suitable to a particular fixture.

Accessibility

Coaches must never be remote and inaccessible. They must be able to relate to players in a positive and friendly way. The job of the coach is to improve the individual, the unit and the overall team performance. Any player who has worries about his own performance – or criticism of selection – should be able to discuss these matters freely with the coach. One of the surest ways to win the confidence and respect of the team is to be available to them to iron out problems.

When choosing a coach, look for one with all or most of the above qualities. He may not actually be on the field of play with you but his preparation will inform everything that you do in a game. If he has been thorough and methodical, it will be clearly seen. If he has glaring faults, they will be soon exposed. Choose your coach very carefully. And search for one with real personality.

Tactics

Tactical superiority wins games and a coach must be a master tactician. There are two basic systems of play in rugby and they produce contrasting philosophies:

(i) The power game, using forward dominance to wear down the oppo sition and gain territorial advantage.

(ii) The expansive game, using the running and handling skills of players.

The All Blacks were the prime exponents of the power game in the 1980s and their juggernaut pack controlled play. France and Fiji have always preferred open, fifteen-man rugby that allows individual talents to be shown to the full. Other international teams have used a judicious mixture of both approaches to the game.

All teams play to their strength and it is up to the coach to exploit that strength to optimum advantage. At the same time, his tactics must take account of the opposition. A well-prepared coach will know the strengths and weaknesses of the opposing team. He can then decide on the best tactics to contain the dangers and to apply pressure where it will be most effective. This may involve a tactical switch from an original game plan.

Tactical switches are not always successful. During the 1991 World Cup matches, England won their way to the final by playing a rugged forward game that was reinforced by the accurate line-kicking of their half-backs. It was controlled rugby of a most effective kind. The Australians, in sharp contrast, had played expansive rugby of a more attractive type. It was full of variety, invention and spectacle. When the teams met in the final, England decided to play the Australians at their own game and threw the ball around in a way they had never done throughout the tournament. The Wallabies duly won the final on their own terms. Many critics felt that England surrendered the game the moment their tactical approach was changed.

Every coach wants his team to function effectively. To make them do this, he has a number of tactical considerations to make. Some of these occur in team selection, with certain players being picked for specific roles in a particular game. But there are many other tactical decisions to make:

(i) An overall game plan.

(ii) Ploys to secure possession at set-pieces and to disrupt the opposition.

(iii) Deciding when to ruck and when to maul.

(iv) Defensive ploys for forwards and backs.

(v) Back-row ploys in attacking situations.

(vi) A repertoire of midfield ploys in attack.

(vii) Deciding how tight or open a game can be.

(viii) Assigning individual roles to players at starts and restarts.

(ix) Attacking ploys from tap penalties.

(x) Knowing when to kick for goal from a penalty.

Many factors can influence the various attacking and defensive ploys and the coach will have taken account of them. His players will thus always know what to do in any given situation. Decisive play speeds up the game and puts pressure on the opposition. A well-coached team will have a tactical awareness that gives them an immediate advantage. They will never take the field without knowing what their overall strategy is. If that strategy proves inadequate then they will have contingency plans to make tactical changes. The industrious coach will have covered all the options.

Sevens

Seven-a-side rugby is one of the most exhilarating versions of the game. Exciting to play and entertaining to watch, it is usually played in tournaments before or after the normal fifteen-a-side seasons. One of the highlights of the rugby calendar is the Hong Kong Sevens where the best teams in the world compete in a festival atmosphere. Teams found wanting in fifteen-a-side rugby can often turn the tables on the victors when it comes to Sevens. The Fijian team has won the Hong Kong Sevens on more than one occasion by defeating the mighty All Blacks or the Wallabies.

Seven-a-side teams play on a full-size pitch. This greatly enlarges the amount of space to cover or exploit. Speed and flair are at a premium. Crisp handling is essential. Solid tackling is crucial. Every player is continually examined by his opponents. His commitment, his basic skills and his ability to improvise are on trial. Though the games are much shorter – seven or ten minutes' duration – they are played at a pace which calls for supreme fitness.

Possession is everything in Sevens. As soon as you have the ball – wherever you may be on the pitch – you are on the attack. The side which controls the movement of the ball can exert a tremendous psychological pressure. Ball retention thus has the highest priority. It is more important to keep possession than to advance upfield so a team may slow the game to a standstill and inter-pass until a mistake or an impetuous move by the opposition gives them a chance to launch an attack.

Good sevens players must have a whole array of skills. They must be:

(i) Exceptionally fit.
(ii) Tireless supporters of the man in possession.

(iii) Outstanding runners with good acceleration.

(iv) Effective ball-winners and secure handlers.

(v) Sound tacklers.

(vi) Quick-thinking with good anticipation.

They must also have the stamina to play consistently well throughout a long tournament and the ability to improvise at short notice. Sevens teams must be well organised and they must always include a reliable goal-kicker.

Positions

The team consists of three forwards and four backs. Each has a specialist position that calls for specific attributes.

Tight-Head Prop

The most powerful of the three forwards. He must be an experienced scrummager who can dominate the opposition and help the hooker to secure good possession.

Hooker

He must be able to strike quickly to win controlled ball at the scrummages. He must also throw the ball in accurately at the lineouts.

Loose-Head Prop

As well as being able to scrummage effect-ively, he must work to secure possession in the transitional phases of play. His function in this respect is akin to that of a flanker in the fifteen-man game. Indeed, a flanker or a number 8 is often selected as the loose-head prop. He is also the specialist jumper in the team and should be capable of securing good possession at lineouts and kick-offs.

All three forwards must be highly mobile and have the handling skills normally associated with a back division.

Scrum-Half

The link between forwards and backs. He must be a good decision-maker who knows when to exploit space by making a break. His service must be accurate and reliable under the most intense pressure.

Outside-Half

He controls the tempo of play when his side have the ball. He will decide the pace and direction of an attack, probing away until a gap finally presents itself. Elusive running skills and qualities of leadership are crucial.

Centre

The most direct and physical of the three-quarters. While he can play a waiting game when in possession, he must have the skills to create a gap in the defence and the power to smash a way through it before releasing a support player.

Wing

The speed merchant with the pace and commitment to evade and outsprint the covering defence. Kicking is limited in Sevens but the well-placed kick ahead can pay handsome dividends if the attacking wing has the pace to get to it first. Once he is put clear anywhere on the field, the wing must have the confidence to go all the way to the try-line. He must also be able to operate with equal facility on the left or the right of the field.

Thorough preparation is mandatory for Sevens and coaches need to organise their training sessions with care. Every aspect of the game must be rehearsed in unopposed

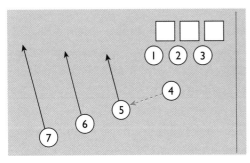

Positions in Sevens
1. Loose head prop.   *5. Outside half.*
2. Hooker.   *6. Centre.*
3. Tight head prop.   *7. Wing.*
4. Scrum half.

and opposed practice sessions until an effective pattern of play is established. But a team strategy must also leave room for individual brilliance and enterprise. Sevens is a game where the magicians of rugby are given full scope.

Kick-Offs and Restarts

Because of the nature of the game, scoring can often be high in Sevens. Restarts from the halfway line recur many times and a strategy for dealing with them must be worked out.

The team receiving the ball must cover as much of the pitch as possible so that they cut down the options available to the opposition. A standard defensive formation is 4-2-1.

A variation of this is the 2-3-2 formation. The fastest two players are the ones at the back because they will have the furthest to run out of the pressure area if they catch the ball.

A third option is the 3-2-2 formation. This closes down the space in a slightly different way.

Most teams have a set mode of defence that suits their particular skills but they must be able to adapt it to the intentions of the opposition at kick-offs or restarts. If a team wishes to secure possession from its own kick-off, the forwards will line up near the touchline and race to the designated landing area of the ball. The defending side must have reorganised itself quickly to cope with this.

The drop-out from the 22-metre line gives the kicker far more options because he can kick the ball from anywhere along the line. He may put in a high kick to the

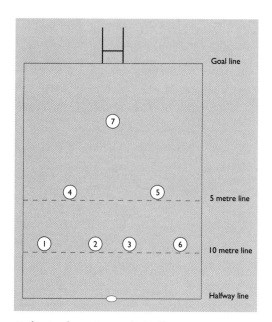

Defensive formations at kick-off
(a) 4 - 2 - 1

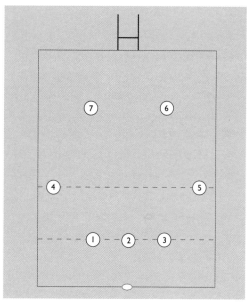

Defensive formations at kick-off
(c) 3 - 2 - 2

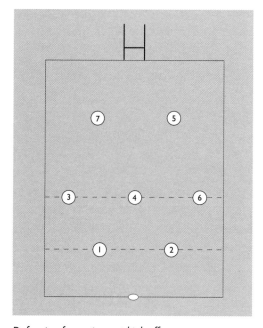

Defensive formations at kick-off
(b) 2 - 3 - 2

touchline for his forwards to run on to; or kick deep into the open space in the opposing half; or kick the ball just over the line so that he can re-gather it instantly and feed a supporting player. A defending side must be alert to all these possibilities and line up accordingly.

Scrums

As a rule, there are more scrums than lineouts in a Sevens match so the importance of the scrum is increased. It is much quicker than the equivalent set-piece in the fifteen-man game so the forwards must be alert and agile.

Props must support their hooker and

drive forward as the ball is put in so that he is able to make a swift strike for the ball. A team should always win the ball on their own put-in. Good communication with the scrum-half is critical. Before the scrum goes down, he will signal what type of ball he expects from the hooker. The props will time their shove to coincide with the ball coming in.

The quality of the possession is controlled by the speed and the strike. Too hard a strike will send the ball shooting out of the scrum. A ball that is hooked too slowly gives the opposition more time to encroach or disrupt. There are two options for the hooker:

(i) Channel one is through the legs of the loose-head prop. This produces quicker ball but needs careful prac-

tice. The prop must have a wide stance to take the strain and offer a clear target area.

(ii) Channel two is through the gap between the non-striking foot of the hooker and the inside foot of the loose-head prop. There is slightly better protection for the scrum-half with this ball. Positioning of the feet is again vital.

The scrum-half will choose which option he prefers at each scrum. On the opposition put-in, the forwards must time their drive to disrupt their opponents and give their own hooker the chance to take the ball against the head. They may also push their opponents off the ball or wheel the scrum to deny them quality possession. Another option

A scrum, showing the wide range of options for the attacking side.

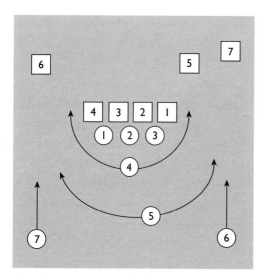

Attacking options at midfield scrummage.

is for the hooker to kick the ball through the legs of the opposing forwards so that his own scrum-half can chase it. As soon as the ball is hooked, the forwards must break from the scrum and become three-quarters. Mobility and support are the watchwords.

The location of each scrum will dictate the positions taken up by the back division. If the scrum is near a touchline then they will line up on the open-side. This leaves the blind-side for the scrum-half to exploit.

If the scrum is in the middle of the field, then the options are increased. The outside-half can go either way with the possibility of support on the inside from either his centre or his wing.

If there is a wide space on the blind-side, it must be covered by the winger.

His speed can be used to bring him into the attack on the open-side.

Signalling of all these ploys must be clear. The defending side must be alert to all the possibilities and able to counter them. Their positioning must allow flexibility.

Lineout

The best attacking opportunities can come from the lineout because the ball is quicker, the opposition has to stand ten metres behind the line of the forwards and there are no marauding flankers to close down the outside-half. Every team should secure the ball on their own throw-in.

Timing and accuracy of the throw are the key factors. The hooker will usually be the thrower but a team with two or more throwers has a distinct advantage. If a winger and a hooker change places at a throw, it will confuse the opposition. When a scrum-half takes the throw-in then runs around to receive the ball, his hooker can become an extra man in the line.

A variety of ploys may be used at the lineout but the code of signals must be clear and unbreakable. The two jumpers must move around and change positions at lineouts in order to keep the opposition guessing. Basic ploys are:

(i) Throwing the ball direct to the first or second jumper so that he can catch it or deflect it down to the jumper.

(ii)   Throwing the ball quickly into the lineout before the opposing jumpers are ready.

(iii) Throwing a long ball to the back of the line to a jumper who deliberately arrives late.

(iv) Stretching the line back so that there is space at the front for the scrum-half to run in and take the ball from the thrower.

(v)   Feinting to move in the line then going in the opposite direction to take the ball.

(vi) Throwing a long ball over the line out for the scrum-half or one of the three-quarters to receive.

If the opposition have the throw-in, the two jumpers must be aware of these and other possible ploys. They will need quick reflexes to counter them and must be through quickly on any bad ball that is delivered to the scrum-half. Once the ball is out, they become additional three-quarters.

Ruck and Maul

There is little rucking in Sevens. Players should not risk going to ground in possession if they can pass to a support player. The ball must be kept alive at all times. If a player is tackled in possession and goes to ground, he must release the ball at once. The nearest player should pick it up and pass it away from the danger area.

Mauls will be quick and small-scale affairs. If too many players commit themselves at a breakdown, they will leave defensive gaps. When a player is held in possession, he should either be able to slip the ball to a colleague or receive physical assistance from the nearest support player who will attempt to wrest the ball from him and pass it out. An additional support player may go into the maul to lend weight and assistance. Once the ball is out, players in the maul must recover their positions.

Tackling

All Sevens players must be resolute tacklers. Speed and positional sense are great assets. A tackle must not just halt the player in possession. Ideally, it should make it impossible for him to pass the ball to a support player. The smother tackle is particularly effective in Sevens, wrapping the arms around the ball-carrier to prevent release and driving him backwards at the same time.

If the ball-carrier is brought to ground, the tackler must try to turn him round so that the ball is presented to the support players from the defending team. Quick recovery from a tackle is important. Get up at once and rejoin the action.

Kicking

Crisp handling is the essence of good Sevens play and the amount of kicking is consequently reduced. Never squander good possession with a kick. Only resort to a kick in open play when it can be really effective. The long kick ahead into space is best used when you have pace in the team to be confident of regaining possession. A diagonal kick from one of the half-backs towards the corner flag may let in a speedy winger for a try. A stout defensive line which comes quickly can be breached with a well-judged chip-kick over their heads. And there may be times when a long kick downfield is needed to relieve sustained pressure near your try-line.

Kick in moderation. Be accurate. Pursue the kick hard.

Penalties

A penalty gives a team its best possession. Do not kick it away by putting the ball into touch. Have a whole repertoire of penalty moves and vary them throughout the game. Speed is the key. The quickly taken tap penalty can catch the defence napping and open up gaps. When the penalty is awarded, the scrum-half must pounce on the ball, give the signal and set the move in motion. He is the decision-maker.

The scrum-half is the fulcrum of all penalty moves. There is an endless variety of ploys he can use. They include:

(i) Looping. The scrum-half passes to the outside-half and loops around him to take the pass and transfer the ball to the centre. The scrum-half can then loop outside the centre to receive the ball again and put his wing away.

(ii) Decoy. The scrum-half passes to the outside-half and loops around him to act as a decoy. The ball is passed to one of the forwards down the blind side, switching the angle of attack completely.

(iii) Lateral move. The scrum-half runs directly across the field in front of his three-quarters and offers the ball to each in turn. He executes a scissors move with the player who is best placed to split open a defence with a straight run.

(iv) Close to the opposition line, the players in attack move further away to give themselves room to build up speed. On a signal from the scrum-half, they all run towards the line, giving him six potential ball-receivers. He taps the ball through the mark and feeds the designated player whose momentum should take him through the cover and over the line.

Other ploys involve more complicated looping, scissors movements, dummies, dummy scissors movements and decoys. If the penalty is taken quickly enough, swift transfer to the wing may be enough to put him clear.

The defending side must therefore regroup themselves instantly when a penalty is awarded so that they provide blanket cover. Their job is to exert maximum pressure on the attackers by coming up quickly on them in formation to limit the amount of space and thinking time. One player must be used to attack and harass the pivotal scrum-half.

Penalty Kicks

These should be rarely taken. Why settle for three possible points when you might score seven? Even kicks right in front of the posts should be scorned because they give the perfect opportunity to use a penalty move. Run the ball and you put the defence under pressure. Opt for the kick and you give them a respite. If the kick fails, the opposition may gain possession and launch a counter-attack.

Penalty kicks may be taken for tactical reasons. If your side is well ahead, it is a way of slowing the game down and allowing them a brief rest. If you have a slender lead in the dying minutes of a game, the kick at goal may eat up precious time as well as gaining three more points.

The goal-kicker really comes into his own when tries are scored. And teams which run the ball intelligently from penalties usually give him plenty of practice.

Discipline

Pace yourselves in a tournament. You may have to play six or seven games in a day and must not exhaust yourself by over-exertion in the early rounds. Learn to slow the game down and to play cat-and-mouse with the opposition. Tournaments usually allow a squad of players. Spread the load throughout the team. Make sure that you have the best and fittest seven players in the final.

Maintain discipline to the final whistle. Even a relatively large lead can be slashed to pieces in Sevens. Three quick tries in the last few minutes can put twenty-one points on the board for the opposition. Control the tempo and flow of the game throughout its duration.

Seven-a-side rugby is not just enormous fun to play and to watch. It is a valuable exercise to use in training to test fitness and sharpen up reactions. It is also an attractive way to introduce newcomers to the game of rugby.

Women's Rugby

The growth of women's rugby in the last decade has been one of the most exciting developments in the game. There has been a veritable explosion of interest. More women are taking up the sport, more teams are being formed and more representative matches are being played. The status and the standard of women's rugby have improved enormously. This is due in some measure to the coaching, refereeing and general encouragement given by rugby men everywhere; but it is chiefly the work of the women themselves. Their attitude towards the game has been exemplary and they have shown ambition and enterprise in the way they have organised it.

Those who came to mock the first Women's Rugby World Cup in April 1991 went away chastened. The twelve national teams who gathered together in South Wales put on a splendid feast of rugby. Sponsorship may have been poor and attendance on the modest side, but the games themselves lacked nothing in skill and commitment. The final was a hard-fought battle between England and the USA with the superior power of the Americans eventually turning the game their way.

In 1994, the second World Cup – renamed the World Championships to avoid confusion with the men's game – was held in Edinburgh. Twelve teams again competed for the honours though the ability gap between some of the XVs was vast. Huge scores were run up in some games and the USA reached the final with an astounding average of 91 points per game. England gained their revenge this time, beating the Americans in the final by 38–23.

With professionalism creeping into the men's game more and more at the top level, it is reassuring to watch international rugby tournaments played in the

England scrum-half Emma Mitchell gets the ball away in the World Championship Final against the USA in 1994. England won the game in style.

right spirit by true amateurs. All the teams paid their own way. They had been brought together by a common love of the game and this shone through both world events. Motivated by national pride, they gave of their best. For everyone involved both on and off the field, the 1991 Women's Rugby World Cup and the 1994 World Championships were wonderful learning experiences.

The game is organised in Britain by the Women's Rugby Football Union. It is run by a national committee which has a number of regional representatives so that all areas of the country have a voice

in the conduct of affairs. The WRFU supervises Club Competitions and Student Competitions. Each comprises a League and a Cup Competition. League titles are awarded on the basis of maximum points (two for a win; one for a draw) secured in any season. There is promotion and relegation between the divisions.

The cup competition for Club and Students takes the form of an annual knockout contest. There is also a National Sevens Tournament at the end of each season. This is a showpiece event and the ideal way for any prospective newcomers to be introduced to the women's game. The flair, fitness and dedication of the teams who take part in this tournament is impressive. Winning finalists will already have played five or six games before they do battle for the trophy.

If you are interested in taking up women's rugby, contact your regional representative. Many of the leading teams are attached to men's clubs – Wasps, Saracens, Richmond, Waterloo and so on – and benefit from shared facilities as well as support and advice. Others exist independently and draw their players from a wide catchment area. There are now well over two hundred women's clubs in existence and plenty of room for more.

Notwithstanding many setbacks, the women's game is thriving and achieving new standards of excellence all the time. Any beginner will be made welcome and taught the rudiments of the game. Rugby is a sport in which you learn fast.

The future lies with the women themselves. They must not simply copy the men's game. Their role models must be female. They have to find their own coaches, their own referees, their own distinctive style of play. The more independent they become, the quicker the game will develop. This does not mean that they jettison male help completely – that would be foolhardy. But women must control and shape their game in the 1990s.

They must recruit vigorously to swell the ranks in the lower reaches of the game. And they must strive to retain the services of those at the top whose playing careers are almost over. Experience is irreplaceable. There is now a whole generation of players in Britain with international or regional honours. It is from amongst these that the top women coaches and referees and administrators will come.

Mini Rugby

Mini Rugby was first introduced in 1970 and it has blossomed in the past twenty-five years. It was designed for youngsters who would not otherwise have had the opportunity of playing rugby; they were introduced to the fifteen-man game by an abbreviated version of it. Fewer players, smaller pitch, shorter matches. The emphasis in Mini Rugby was put on running, handling, passing and support play. Tackling was a feature of the game for all ages until 1990. The decision was then made to make the under-nine game strictly a non-contact one. It was a controversial move but it had sound thinking behind it. Injuries were minimised and newcomers to the sport were not haunted by the fear of contact. They were able to find their feet in the game before those feet could legitimately be tackled from under them.

Mini Rugby is played between teams of various sizes. Pitches are reduced in size for different age groups. Boys under ten are recommended to play on a pitch measuring 59 metres by 28 metres. Boys under thirteen play on a pitch measuring 69 metres by 38 metres. It is usual to play across a full-size rugby pitch with use being made of existing lines. The goal-line must not be used as one of the touchlines because of the danger of players running into the posts.

Rules

The kick-off is from the centre of the field and drop-outs are taken on or behind the existing 15-metre line. The under-eights should be allowed to use a place-kick.

Direct kicking to touch is only allowed from within the 15-metre area. Dribbling is allowed but fly-kicking – wild hacking of the ball – is illegal anywhere on the field. The opposition will be awarded a

Starting early: nine-year-olds get a taste of Mini Rugby.

scrum at the point of the kick.

Tapped penalties at the place of the kick are awarded to the opposition when a kick from between the 15-metre lines goes directly into touch. The tapped penalty is taken at the point from which the ball was kicked. The opposition should retire at least seven metres from the place of infringement.

Tackling is restricted to players of ten years or over.

There are no lineouts for the under-eights. They are replaced by a scrum ten metres in from the touchline.

The scrum-half must not follow his opposite number around the scrum until the ball is out or he will concede a tapped penalty to the opposition.

Scoring is conventional, although conversion kicks are taken in front of the posts for the under-nines and under-tens; they are waived altogether for the under-eights. For boys of eleven and over, the conversion is as normal.

All the laws of off-side, on-side, knock-on, throw-forward and so on, apply as usual.

Playing time depends on circumstances. Fifteen minutes each way is suitable for all groups of ten and under.

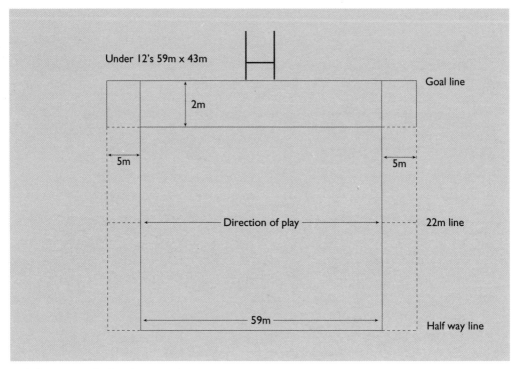

Under 12's 59m x 43m

2m

5m

5m

Direction of play

59m

Goal line

22m line

Half way line

Pitch for Mini Rugby for players under 13.

Twenty minutes each way may be played by those of eleven and over.

Mini Rugby is the ideal way to learn and appreciate the game of rugby. Midi Rugby, for older boys, is a twelve-a-side game which is the stepping stone to the full fifteen-a-side adult game. At a young age, players become conversant with the basic skills of the game – running, handling, contact and support play. They will learn how to exploit space and they will also understand the importance of team spirit. Four principles will be established – Go Forward, Support, Continuity and Pressure. Youngsters must master

these principles before they can progress to the adult game.

Like all rugby, Mini Rugby should be properly coached and supervised. Teams must be well-matched. Tournaments must be carefully structured. Above all else, Mini Rugby stresses the fun element of the game. Winning or losing do not have the significance they hold in the senior game. Taking part is the key factor. The players must enjoy rugby for its own sake, build their self-confidence and develop team spirit.

Boys have boundless enthusiasm and learn fast. Catch them young, teach them

Five-a-side
Forwards: Prop Hooker
Backs: Scrum-half Outside-half Centre

Seven-a-side
Forwards: Prop Hooker Prop
Backs: Scrum-half Outside-half Centre Centre

Nine-a-side
Forwards: Prop Hooker Prop
Backs: Scrum-half Outside-half Centre Centre
Wing Wing

Twelve-a-side
Forwards: Prop Lock Hooker Prop Lock
Backs: Scrum-half Outside-half Centre Centre
Wing Wing Full back

Positions in Mini Rugby.

properly and they may be committed to the game for life. Thanks to a huge voluntary effort by clubs and parents, Mini Rugby teams exist all over Britain. There are variations. In Wales, it is now called Dragon Rugby. Ireland calls it Leprechaun Rugby. The Australians prefer Walla Rugby while the New Zealanders use the term New Image. Whatever name used for Mini Rugby, it is a vital way of injecting new blood into the game. It is from the ranks of these players that the future stars of fifteen-a-side rugby will eventually come.

Refereeing

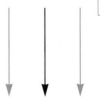

The job of the referee is to control the game and enforce the laws with fairness and firmness. Referees will never be universally popular but they are crucial figures in any match. A game that is not supervised by a referee will soon descend into an uncontrolled shambles. Partisan supporters will always have partisan opinions and even the most just decisions of a referee will be greeted by howls of derision. Referees must learn to live with this. They must stand by their decisions and not be swayed by any crowd dissent.

The good referee must have a clear understanding of the game and a sound knowledge of the laws. If he has played rugby himself, he will have a valuable insight into the minds and actions of players. What both teams will want from him is clarity, consistency and control.

A confused referee is a walking hazard. An inconsistent one will stir up frustration and dissent. A weak one is a

real disaster. The ideal referee is largely invisible. He is so completely in charge that he does not need attention-seeking behaviour to reinforce that fact. He will try to keep the game flowing and avoid unnecessary stoppages. Infringements will be dealt with promptly and fairly. His decisions will be impartial and clearly signalled. He must have a natural skill in man management and good-humoured diplomacy.

Referees need a high level of fitness and a good sense of positioning. They must be in the right position to spot any infringements but they must not interfere with play. If there are any flash-points, they must move in rapidly to defuse the situation. If two players fight, they can be given stern individual warnings and allowed time to cool down. If a more general brawl develops, the referee must call the captains and warn them jointly that the next offender will be sent from

Welsh referee Derek Bevan keeps a firm hand on the World Cup Final, 1991.

the field. He must not hesitate to dismiss a persistent offender no matter what intimidation he receives.

The whistle halts the game and the signal explains the decision. But a good referee will also talk to the players throughout the game. He will justify his decisions with polite firmness. His manner can also help to set the tone of the game. A nit-picking, whistle-happy referee is a pain to players and spectators alike. The referee who patently enjoys the game and who polices it in the right spirit can make it a much more satisfactory event for all concerned. Judicious use of the advantage law is a factor here. The good referee will try to keep the game alive whenever possible.

Players

Players must not see the referee as an enemy. He is there to exercise control and that will help both sides. He will also reduce the risk of serious injury by jumping in to stop any outbreaks of violence.

All referees make mistakes. Even the best of them can be unsighted and miss infringements. At the lineout, there are so many potential infringements that no referee can spot and punish them all. He will select the most glaring and take appropriate action.

Play to the whistle. Dissent is always a waste of time and will be punished. If a referee makes a bad decision, accept it with grace and get on with the game. No referee will change a decision because a player yells at him. If a player disputes the validity of a penalty or a free kick, he will concede another ten metres of territory to the opposition.

Every referee has his own interpretation of the laws. Players must be able to adjust to each individual. This is especially the case at international level where the differences of interpretation between countries can be quite marked. Touring parties to distant lands may find themselves penalised for offences that are treated more leniently at home. Instead of disputing the new interpretation, they must adapt their style of play to take account of it.

Referees are human beings. They perform an invaluable function and must be included in post-match socialising. Teams must never ostracise a referee because he may have inadvertently given a bad decision against them. Players should use every opportunity to talk to referees and learn to appreciate the game from their viewpoint.

Persistent dissenters are a handicap in any team. One way to check their routine protests is to give them experience of refereeing on the practice field. Even ten minutes in charge of a game will alter their attitude. They will come to appreciate just how much ground a referee has to cover and how vigilant he has to be. They will also understand some of the other problems with which he has to contend on a regular basis. Always treat referees with respect. It is a highly important aspect of the self-discipline needed on a rugby field.

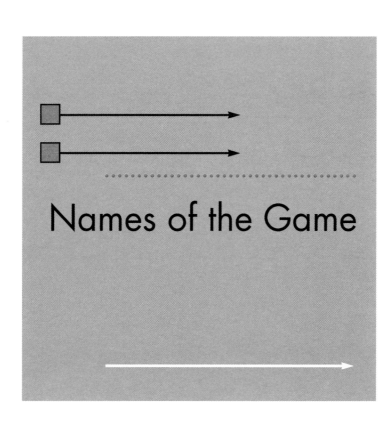

Names of the Game

Glossary

Advantage Law The discretion of the referee to allow play to continue after an infringement in case the non-offending team can gain a greater advantage than they would from a stoppage.

All Blacks The touring New Zealand team.

Ankle Tap A method of bringing down the ball-carrier by tapping his ankle to knock him off balance. The tap must be done with a hand. Tripping with a foot is illegal.

Attacking Team The team in their opponents' half of the field.

Backs The back division consists of those players who take up their position behind the scrum.

Blind-Side The narrow side, nearer to a touchline. The opposite side of the field to where the backs line up from a scrum, lineout, ruck or maul.

Blind-Side Flanker Wing-forward who packs down on the blind side of the scrum.

Charge Down The blocking of an opponent's kick with the hands, arms or body. If the ball touches the ground, it is not a knock-on.

Conversion A successful kick over the crossbar following a try. The kick is taken from a mark in line with the point where the try was taken. It will be placed as far downfield as the kicker chooses. If the kick goes over, the try is converted to a goal. The kick is worth two points.

Dead The ball is dead when not in play. It may be put into touch or go out over the dead-ball line at either end of the playing area.

Defending Team The team in whose half of the field play comes to a stop.

Drawing a Man Directing your run towards an opponent and committing him before you pass. He will then not be able to harass the ball-receiver.

Dribbling Controlled kicking of the ball along the ground, soccer-style. It is a lost art in modern rugby but was a salient feature of the game at one time.

Drop Kick This is made by dropping the ball from the hands and kicking it on the first rebound after it touches the ground.

Drop-Out A method of restarting play from either the 22-metre line or the centre-spot by means of a drop kick.

Dropped Goal A goal scored from a drop kick in open play, as opposed to a place kick from the ground.

Dummy Pretending to pass to another player but retaining the ball. This is 'selling a dummy' and can create an opening if the defender is deceived and 'buys' it.

Fair Catch If a player catches the ball while he is stationary and in his own 22-metre area, he can shout 'Mark!' to signal a fair catch. He may catch the ball from a kick, knock-on or throw forward by an opponent but one foot must be on the ground. A free kick is awarded for a fair catch. He must kick the ball through the point where he marked it.

Flankers The two back-row forwards who pack down on the flanks of the scrum and have the best chance to leave it quickly and get to the loose ball.

Fly-Half Another name for the outside-half.

Foot-Up When a hooker advances a foot too early in a scrummage and concedes a penalty.

Forward A player who packs down in the scrum or forms part of the lineout. There are eight forwards in a team.

Forward Pass An illegal pass that goes in front of the man passing it. The ball-receiver must take the ball behind the passer or an infringement has occurred.

Free Kick A kick awarded for a fair catch or to the non-offending team after certain infringements. A goal cannot be scored directly from a free kick unless the ball has first been played by another player. A free kick may be taken in any form – punt, drop-kick or place kick.

Front-Row The two props and the hooker who form the front-row of a scrum.

Full-Back The last line of defence, taking up his position behind the three-quarters. He can be used in attack if he comes into the line to make the extra man. He is often the team's goal-kicker.

Garryowen An up-and-under named after the famous Irish club.

Goal The combination of a try and successful conversion, now worth seven points.

Grand Slam Winning all four games in the Home International Championship. By defintion, this will also include winning the Triple Crown.

Grubber Kick A kick from the hands that travels along the ground, rolling over on its head.

Half-Backs The scrum-half and outside-half.

Hand-Off A way of fending off a tackler by pushing him away with the palm of the hand.

Hooker The forward in the middle of the scrum whose job is to hook the ball out with his foot.

Interception Seizing a pass that is aimed by an opposition player to a colleague. An interception demands timing. The intercepting player must not be off-side at the moment when the ball is released.

Kick-Off A place kick from the centre of the halfway line. This starts off each period of play in both halves of a game.

Knock-On When the ball bounces forward off the hand or arm of the player trying to catch or pick it up. If it bounces sideways or backwards, it is not a knock-on. If the ball is adjusted as it is caught, it is not a knock-on.

Line-of-Touch An imaginary line on the field of play at right angles to the touchline through the place where the ball is to be thrown at a lineout.

Lineout The line formed by both sets of forwards for a throw-in when the ball has gone into touch. A one-metre gap must be kept between the teams and the ball must be thrown in straight.

Lions Name given to the touring British Isles team. To become a British Lion is the highest honour in the British game.

Lock-Forwards The two second-row forwards.

Loose-Head Prop The prop who packs down with his head outside that of his opposite number and thus free. The

ball will be put in by his own scrum-half on that side because his hooker will be closer to it when it comes in.

Mark (i) The mark is the place on the pitch at which a free kick or penalty is awarded and it will be signalled by the referee, digging in his heel.
(ii) It is also the call made by a player who is making a fair catch.

Maul A scrummage of players from both teams made around a player carrying the ball. If he drops the ball to the ground, the maul becomes a ruck.

Number 8 The forward who scrums down at the back of the scrum. He wears number 8 on his jersey and forms the back-row with the two flankers.

Off-Side A player is off-side is he is in front of the ball when it is kicked, passed or is being carried by a member of his own team.

Open-Side The side of the scrum that is further away from the touchline and hence the one most likely to be exploited by the attacking side.

Open-Side Flanker The wing-forward who packs down on the open-side of a scrum.

Outside-Half The back who acts as a link between the scrum-half and the rest of the back division.

Overlap When the team in possession has more players in attack than the defence has, they create an overlap and thus put their outside man away.

Pack The forwards. They pack down in the scrum.

Pack Captain Leader of the forwards. He may also be the team captain but is not necessarily so.

Penalty Goal A goal scored from a penalty is worth three points.

Penalty Kick Awarded for an infringement of the laws. The non-offending team may kick for goal if they are within range; or they may kick for touch or employ a tactical kick. The penalty may take the form of a punt, a drop kick or a place kick. A tap kick may also be taken to initiate a passing movement.

Penalty Try At his discretion, the referee can award a penalty try if a player is fouled or impeded when a try would probably have been scored. All conversion attempts for a penalty try are taken in front of the posts.

Place Kick When the ball is kicked from the ground after it has been specifically placed there. It is stood upright in a trough made by the kicker's heel or in a mound of sand brought on for the purpose. In windy conditions, the ball may be steadied by a team-mate who lies on the ground alongside it.

Prop-Forwards The two front-row forwards on either side of the hooker.

Punt A kick from the hands. The ball is dropped straight on to the boot.

Replacement A substitute player allowed on to the field as a replacement for an injured team-mate. Tactical substitution is not allowed in rugby. An injury must be genuine before a player is allowed to leave the game.

Ruck A scrummage formed by both sets of forwards after the ball has gone to ground in open play.

Scrum-Half The inside-half who links the forwards with the backs. He monitors the scrums and the lineouts and makes all the key decisions about use of possession.

Scrummage A scrummage or scrum is a means of restarting play after an infringement. Eight players from each side normally form a scrum in 3-4-1 formation. The two sets of front-row forwards interlock with each other.

Second-Row The two forwards who form the second-row of the scrum and who are the specialist jumpers in the lineout.

Set-Pieces The scrum and the lineout.

Sevens Seven-a-side rugby is played on a full-size pitch with seven players on each side. Games are greatly reduced in length so that teams can play a number of games in knock-out tournaments. It is a fast, open type of rugby that calls for maximum fitness.

Springboks The touring South African team.

Stand-Off Half Another name for the outside-half, who is described above.

Tackle Stopping an opponent who is carrying the ball by tackling him.

Tap Kick This is made after a restart. A kick of only a few inches made by a player to himself so that he can run the ball, pass or kick it.

Three-Quarters The two centres and the two wings.

Throw Forward Official name for a forward pass.

Tight-Head Prop The prop who packs down with his head between that of the opposing hooker and loose-head prop.

Touch-Down If a defending player grounds the ball in his own in-goal area, it is a touch-down and not a try. If an opponent has put the ball over the try-line, there is a drop-out from the 22-metre line. If the defender has carried the ball over his own line before grounding it, he concedes a five-metre scrum to the opposition.

Touch-in-Goal When the ball goes out of play behind the goal-line.

Touchline The two lines down either side of the pitch. Any ball that touches the line or the ground beyond it is said to be in touch.

Triple Crown If one of the four home countries defeats the other three in a season's international championship, they hold the Triple Crown. It is a mythical trophy but coveted nevertheless.

Try When a player grounds the ball in an opponents' in-goal area, he scores a try.

It is now worth five points. All tries are followed by attempted conversions. If a kick is successful, the try becomes a goal.

Units Some teams like to divide up into mini-units for training purposes. They can do specialist work on the Front-Five (front-row and second-row); on the Back-Row (number 8 and flankers); on the Back-Five (back-row and half-backs); on the Half-Backs themselves (scrum-half and outside-half); on the Midfield (the two centres); and on the Back-Three (full-back and two wings).

Up-and-Under A high tactical kick used to put pressure on the opposing team. While the ball is in the air, the team-mates of the kicker will chase it hard to tackle the ball-catcher as he receives it. This can be especially effective in wet conditions that make handling very difficult; or when the sun is in the eyes of the potential ball-receiver.

Wallabies The Australian Rugby Team.

Wheel A scrummaging manoeuvre where the scrum is wheeled to gain advantage. On their own ball, a pack may wheel to set up a back-row move. On opposition ball, a pack may wheel suddenly to disrupt the scrum. If a scrummage wheels through an angle of 90 degrees then it must be taken again.

Wing-Forward Another name for flanker.

Wing Three-Quarters The two outside backs who are usually the fastest men in the team.

Laws of the Game

as framed by the International Rugby Football Board

LAW 1 (THE GROUND); LAW 2 (THE BALL); LAW 3 (NUMBER OF PLAYERS); LAW 4 (PLAYERS' DRESS); LAW 5 (TOSS, TIME); AND LAW 6 (REFEREE AND TOUCH JUDGES) HAVE ALREADY BEEN COVERED IN EARLIER SECTIONS OF THIS BOOK.

Law 7. Mode of Play

A match is started by a kick-off, after which any player who is on-side and provided he does so in accordance with these Laws may at any time:

* catch or pick up a ball and run with it
* pass, throw or knock a ball to another player
* kick or otherwise propel the ball
* tackle, push or shoulder an opponent holding the ball
* fall on the ball
* take part in scrummage, ruck, maul or lineout
* ground the ball in In-goal.

Law 8. Advantage

The referee shall not whistle for any infringement during play which is followed by an advantage gained by the non-offending team. An advantage must be either territorial or such possession of the ball as constitutes an obvious tactical advantage. A mere opportunity to gain advantage is not sufficient.

Law 9. Ball or Player Touching Referee

(1) If the ball or player carrying it touches the referee in the field-of-play, play shall continue unless the referee considers either team has gained an advantage in which case he shall order a scrummage. The team which last played the ball shall put it in.

(2) (a) If the ball in a player's possession or a player carrying it touches the

referee in that player's In-goal, a touchdown shall be awarded.

(b) If a player carrying a ball in his opponents' In-goal touches the referee before grounding the ball, a try shall be awarded at that place.

Law 10. Kick-Off

Kick-off is (a) a place kick taken from the centre of the halfway line by the team which has the right to start the match or by the opposing team on the resumption of play after the half-time interval; or (b) a drop kick taken at or from behind the centre of the halfway line by the defending team after the opposing side has scored.

(1) The ball must be kicked from the correct place and by the correct form of kick; otherwise it shall be kicked off again.

(2) The ball must reach the opponent's ten-metre line, unless first played by an opponent; otherwise, it shall be kicked off again or a scrummage formed at the centre, at the opposition's option. If it reaches the ten-metre line and is then blown back, play shall continue.

(3) If the ball is kicked directly into touch, the opposing team may accept the kick, have the ball kicked off again, or have a scrummage formed at the centre.

(4) If the ball crosses the opposing team's goal-line from a kick-off, without touch-

ing or being touched by a player, the opposing team has the option of grounding the ball, making it dead or playing on. If the opposing team grounds the ball or makes it dead or the ball becomes dead by touch-in-goal or by touching or crossing the dead-ball line, they will have the option of either having the scrummage formed at the centre of the halfway line, with the put-in, or having the other team kick-off again.

(5) The *kicker's team* must be behind the ball when kicked otherwise a scrummage shall be formed at the centre.

(6) The *opposing team* must stand on or behind the ten-metre line. If they are in front of that line or if they charge before the ball has been kicked, it shall be kicked off again.

Law 11. Method of Scoring

Discussed earlier in this book.

Law 12. Try and Touch-Down

Grounding the ball is the act of a player who:

(a) while holding the ball in his hand (or hands) or arm (or arms) brings the ball in contact with the ground, or

(b) while the ball is on the ground either:
  * places his hand (or hands) or arm (or arms) on it with downward pressure
  * falls upon it and the ball is anywhere

under the front of his body from waist to neck inclusive.
Picking up the ball from the ground is not grounding it.

A. Try

(1) A player who is on-side scores a try when:
* he carries the ball into his opponents' In-goal; or
* the ball is in his opponents' In-goal.

(2) The scoring of a try includes the following cases:

(a) if a player carries, passes, knocks or kicks the ball into his In-goal and an opponent first grounds it

(b) if, at a scrummage or ruck, a team is pushed over the goal-line and before the ball has emerged it is first grounded in In-goal by an attacking player

(c) if the momentum of a player, when tackled, carries him into the opponents' In-goal and he there grounds the ball

(d) if a player first grounds the ball on his opponents' goal-line or if the ball is in contact with the ground and a goal-post

(e) if a tackle occurs in such a position that the tackled player whilst complying with the Law is able to place the ball on or over the goal-line.

(3) If a player grounds the ball in his opponents' In-goal and picks it up again, a try is scored where it was first grounded.

(4) A try may be scored by a player who is in touch or in touch-in-goal provided he is not carrying the ball.

B. Penalty Try

A penalty try shall be awarded between the posts if but for foul play by the defending team:
* a try would probably have been scored; or
* it would probably have been scored in a more favourable position than where the ball was grounded.

C. Touch-Down

(1) A touch-down occurs when a player first grounds the ball in his In-goal.

(2) After a touch-down play shall be re-started either by a drop-out or a scrummage.

D. Scrummage after Grounding in Case of Doubt

Where there is doubt as to which team first grounded the ball in the In-goal, a scrummage shall be formed five metres from the goal-line opposite the place where the ball was grounded. The attacking team shall put in the ball.

Law 13. Kick at Goal after a Try

(1) After a try has been scored, the scoring team has the right to take a place kick or drop kick at goal, on a line through the place where the try was scored.

(2) If a kick is taken:

(a) it must be taken without undue delay

(b) any player including the kicker may place the ball

(c) the kicker's team except the placer, must be behind the ball when kicked

(d) if the kicker kicks the ball from a placer's hands without the ball being on the ground, the kick is void

(e) the opposing team must be behind the goal-line until the kicker begins his run or offers to kick when they may charge or jump with a view to preventing a goal.

(3) Neither the kicker nor a placer shall wilfully do anything which may lead the opposing team to charge prematurely. If either does so, the charge shall not be disallowed.

Law 14. In-Goal

In-goal is the area bounded by the goal-line, touch-in-goal lines and dead-ball line. It includes the goal-line and goal-posts but excludes touch-in-goal or the dead-ball line.

Touch-in-goal occurs when the ball or player carrying it touches a cornerpost or a touch-in-goal line or the ground or a person or object on or beyond it. The flag is not part of the cornerpost.

Five-Metre Scrummage

(1) A five-metre scrummage is a scrummage formed five metres from the goal-line opposite the place where the ball became dead In-goal but no closer than five metres from the touchline. The attacking team shall put in the ball.

(2) If a player carrying the ball in In-goal is so held that he cannot ground the ball, the ball becomes dead.

(3) A five-metre scrum shall be formed:

(a) If a defending player heels, kicks, carries, passes or knocks the ball into his In-goal, and it there becomes dead without an infringement having occurred, except where:

* a try is scored; or

* he wilfully knocks or throws the ball from the field-of-play into the touch-in-goal or over his dead-ball line; or

(b) if a defending player carrying the ball in the field-of-play is forced into his In-goal and he then touches down; or

(c) if, at a scrummage or ruck a defending team, with the ball in its possession, is pushed over its goal-line and before the ball has emerged first grounds it in In-goal.

(4) Except where the ball is knocked or thrown forward in the field of play or in In-goal, if an attacking player kicks, carries, passes or charges down the ball from his opponents' kick and it travels into his opponents' In-goal either directly or having touched the defender who does not wilfully attempt to stop, catch or kick, and it is there:

* grounded by a defending player; or

* goes into touch-in-goal or over the dead-ball line:

a drop out shall be awarded.

Law 15. Drop out

A drop out is a drop kick awarded to the defending team.

(1) The drop kick must be taken from anywhere on or behind the twenty-two metres line; otherwise the ball shall be dropped out again.

(2) The ball must cross the twenty-two metres line, otherwise the opposing team may have it dropped out again, or have a scrummage formed at the centre of the twenty-two metres line. If it crosses the twenty-two metres line and is then blown back, play shall continue.

(3) If a ball is kicked directly into touch, the opposing team may accept the kick, have the ball dropped out again or have a scrummage formed at the centre of the twenty-two metres line.

(4) The *kicker's team* must be behind the ball when kicked otherwise a scrummage shall be formed at the centre of the twenty-two metres line.

(5) The *opposing team* must not charge over the twenty-two metres line; other-wise the ball shall be dropped out again.

Law 16. Fair-Catch (Mark)

(a) A player makes a fair-catch when in his twenty-two metre area of his In-goal, he having at least one foot on the ground, cleanly catches the ball direct from a kick by one of his opponents, and, at the same time, he exclaims 'Mark!'

A fair catch may be obtained even though the ball on its way touches a goal-post or crossbar and can be made In-goal.

(b) A free kick is awarded for a fair catch.

(1) The kick must be taken by the player making the fair catch, unless he is injured in so doing. If he is unable to take the kick within one minute a scrummage shall be formed at the mark. His team shall put in the ball.

(2) If the mark is In-goal, the resultant scrummage shall be five metres from the goal-line on a line through the mark.

Law 17. Knock-on or Throw-forward

A knock-on occurs when the ball travels forward towards the direction of the opponents' dead-ball line after:

* a player loses possession of it; or
* a player propels or strikes it with his hand or arm; or
* it strikes a player's hand or arm and touches the ground or another player before it is recovered by the player.

A throw-forward occurs when a player carrying the ball throws or passes it in the direction of the opponents' dead-ball line. A throw-in from touch is not a throw-forward. If the ball is not thrown or passed forward but it bounces forward after hitting a player on the ground, it is not a throw-forward.

(1) The knock-on or throw-forward must not be *intentional*.

(2) If the knock-on or throw-forward is *unintentional*, a scrummage shall be formed at the place of the infringement or, if it occurs at a lineout, fifteen metres from the touch line along the line-of-touch unless:

* the ball is knocked on by a player who is in the act of charging down the kick of an opponent but is not attempting to catch the ball; or
* the ball is knocked on one or more times by a player who is in the act of catching or picking it up or losing possession of it and is recovered by that player before it has touched the ground or another player.

Law 18. Tackle, Lying with, on or near the Ball

A tackle occurs when the player carrying the ball is held by one or more opponents so that he is brought to the ground or the ball comes into contact with the ground. If the ball carrier is on one knee, or both knees, or is sitting on the ground, or is on top of another player who is on the

ground, the ball carrier is deemed to have been brought to the ground.

(1)(a) A tackled player *must immediately* pass the ball

or

release the ball

and

get up or move away from the ball.

(b) After a tackle any other player must be on his feet when he plays the ball.

(c) A player who goes to ground and gathers the ball or with the ball in his possession but who is not tackled must immediately get up on his feet with the ball

or

pass the ball

or

release the ball

and

get up or move away from the ball.

(2) It is illegal for any player:

(a) to prevent a tackled player from passing or releasing the ball, or getting up or moving away after he has passed or released it

(b) to pull the ball from a tackled player's possession or attempt to pick up the ball before the tackled player has released it

(c) while lying on the ground after a tackle to play or interfere with the ball in any way or to tackle or attempt to tackle an opponent carrying the ball

(d) to wilfully fall on or over a player

lying on the ground with the ball in his possession

(e) to wilfully fall on or over players lying on the ground with the ball between them, or in close proximity; or

(f) while lying on the ball in close proximity to the ball to prevent an opponent from gaining possession of it.

(3) A player must not fall on or over a ball emerging from a scrummage or ruck.

(4) A try may be scored if the momentum of a player carries him into the opponents' In-goal even though he is tackled.

Law 19. Lying with, on or near the Ball

The requirements of this law are now incorporated into Law 18.

Law 20. Scrummage

A scrummage, which can take place only in the field-of-play, is formed by players from each team closing up in readiness to allow the ball to be put on the ground between them but is not formed within five metres of the touchline. If the ball in a scrummage is on or over the goal-line the scrummage is ended.

The middle player in each front-row is the hooker and players on either side of him are the props.

The middle-line means an imaginary line on the ground directly beneath the line formed by the junction of the shoulders of the two front-rows.

Forming a Scrummage

(1) A team must not wilfully delay the forming of a scrummage. A free kick will be awarded to the opposing team.

(2) Every scrummage shall be formed at the place of infringement or as near as is practicable within the field-of-play. It must be stationary with the middle-line parallel to the goal lines until the ball has been put in.

Before commencing engagement each front-row must be in a crouched position with heads and shoulders no lower than their hips and so that they are within one arm's length of the opponents' shoulders.

(3) It is dangerous play for a front-row to form-down some distance from its opponents and rush against them.

(4) A minimum of five players from each team shall be required to form a scrummage. While the scrummage is in progress a minimum of five players shall remain bound on the scrummage until it ends. Each front-row shall have three players in it at all times. The head of a player in the front row shall not be next to the head of a player in the same team.

(5)(a) While a scrummage is forming:

  * the shoulders of each player in the front-row must not be lower than his hips
  * all players in each front-row must adopt a normal stance

* both feet must be on the ground and not crossed
* a hooker's feet must not be in front of the forward feet of his props.

(b) While the scrummage is taking place, players in each front-row must have their weight firmly on at least one foot and be in a position for an effective forward shove and the shoulders of each player must not be lower than his hips.

(c) When five players of a team form the scrummage the two players in the second-row must remain bound to each other until the scrummage ends.

Binding of Players

(6)(a) The players of each front-row shall bind firmly and continuously while the scrummage is forming, while the ball is being put in and while it is in the scrummage.

(b) The hooker may bind either over or under the arm of his props but, in either case, he must bind firmly around their bodies at or below the level of the armpits. The props must bind the hooker similarly. The hooker must not be supported so that he is not carrying any weight on either foot.

(c) The outside (loose-head) prop *must* either (i) bind his opposing (tight-head) prop with his left arm inside the right arm of his opponent, or (ii) place his left hand or forearm on his left thigh. The tight-head prop *must* bind with his right arm outside the left upper arm of his opposing loose-head prop. He may grip the jersey of his opposing loose-head prop with his right hand but only to keep himself and the scrummage steady and he must not exert a downward pull.

(d) All players in a scrummage, other than those in the front-row, must bind with at least arm and hand round the body of another player of the same team.

(e) No outside player other than a prop may hold an opponent with his outer arm.

Putting a Ball into the Scrummage

(7) When an infringement occurs, the team not responsible shall put in the ball. In all other circumstances, unless otherwise provided, the ball shall be put in by the team which was moving forward prior to the stoppage or, if neither team was moving forward, by the attacking team.

(8) The ball shall be put in without delay as soon as the two front-rows have closed together. A team must put in the ball when ordered to do so and on the side first chosen.

(9) The player putting in the ball shall:

(a) stand one metre from the scrummage and midway between the two front-rows

(b) hold the ball with both hands midway between the two front-rows at a level midway between his knee and ankle

(c) from that position put in the ball:

* without any delay or feint or backward movement, i.e. with a single forward movement; and

* at a quick speed straight along the middle-line so that it first touches the ground immediately beyond the width of the nearer prop's shoulders.

(10) Play in the scrummage begins when the ball leaves the hands of the player putting it in.

(11) If the ball is put in and it comes out at either end of the tunnel, it shall be put in again, unless a free kick or penalty kick has been awarded. If the ball comes out otherwise than at the tunnel, and if a penalty kick has not been awarded, play shall proceed.

Restrictions on Front-Row Players

(12) All front-row players must place their feet so as to allow a clear tunnel. A player must not prevent the ball being put into the scrummage, or from touching the ground at the required place.

(13) No front-row player may raise or advance a foot until the ball has left the hands of the player putting it into the scrummage.

(14) When the ball has touched the ground, any foot of any player in the front-row may be used in an attempt to gain possession of the ball subject to the following:

Players in the front-row must not *at any time* during the scrummage, wilfully:

(a) raise both feet off the ground at the same time; or

(b) adopt a position or take any action, by twisting or lowering the body or by pulling on an opponent's dress, which is likely to cause the scrummage to collapse; or

(c) lift an opponent off his feet or force him upwards out of the scrummage; or

(d) kick the ball out of the tunnel in the direction from which it is put in.

Restrictions on Players

(15) Any player who is not in either front-row must not play the ball while it is in the tunnel.

(16) A player must not:

(a) return the ball to the scrummage; or

(b) handle the ball in the scrummage except in the act of obtaining a 'push over' try or touchdown; or

(c) pick up the ball in the scrummage by hand or legs; or

(d) wilfully collapse the scrummage; or

(e) wilfully fall or kneel in the scrummage; or

(f) attempt to gain possession of the ball in the scrummage with any part of the body except the foot or lower leg.

(17)(a) The player putting in the ball and

his immediate opponent must not kick the ball while it is in the scrummage.

(b) Neither of the players referred to in (a) should take any action while the ball is in the scrummage to convey to the opponent that the ball is out of the scrummage.

(18) A scrummage must not be wheeled beyond a position where the middle-line becomes parallel to the touchline. The scrummage will be reformed at the site of the stoppage, the ball to be put in by the side that has gained possession or otherwise by the same team.

Penalty:

(a) For an infringement of paragraphs (1), (2), (4), (5), (6) (d) and (e), (8), (9), (12), (13), (14) (d), (15), (16) (a) and (f), and (17) (a) and (b), a free kick at the place of the infringement.

(b) For an infringement of paragraphs (3), (6) (a) (b) and (c), (14) (a) (b) and (c), or (16) (b) (c) (d) and (e), a penalty kick at the place of infringement.

Law 21. Ruck

A ruck, which can take place only in the field-of-play, is formed when the ball is on the ground and one or more players from each team are on their feet and in physical contact, closing around the ball between them. If the ball in a ruck is on

or over the goal-line the ruck is ended.

(1) A player joining a ruck must have his head and shoulders no lower than his hips. He must bind with at least one arm round the body of a player of his team in the ruck.

(2) A player must not:

(a) return the ball into the ruck; or

(b) handle the ball in the ruck except in the act of securing a try or touch-down; or

(c) pick up the ball in the ruck by hand or leg; or

(d) wilfully collapse the ruck; or

(e) jump on top of other players in the ruck; or

(f) wilfully fall or kneel in the ruck; or

(g) while lying on the ground interfere in any way with the ball in or emerging from the ruck. He must do his best to roll away from it.

(3) When a ball in a ruck becomes unplayable a scrummage shall be ordered and the ball put in by the team moving forward immediately prior to the formation of the ruck. When neither team was moving forward or where the referee is unable to determine which team was moving forward, the ball shall be put in by the attacking team.

Law 22. Maul

A maul, which can take place only in the field-of-play, is formed by one or more players from each team on their feet and in physical contact closing round the player who is in possession of the ball. A maul ends when the ball is on the ground or the ball or a player carrying it emerges from the maul or when a scrummage is ordered. If the ball in a maul is on or over the goal-line the maul is ended.

(1) A player joining a maul must have his head and shoulders no lower than his hips.

(2) A player must not:

(a) jump on top of players in a maul

(b) wilfully collapse a maul

(c) attempt to drag another player out of a maul.

(3) A player is not in physical contact unless he is caught or bound to the maul and not merely alongside it.

(4)(a) When a maul becomes stationary or the ball in a maul becomes unplayable a scrummage shall be ordered and the ball shall be put in by the team NOT in possession at the commencement of the maul, except where the referee is unable to determine which team was in possession then the ball shall be put in by the team which was moving forward prior to the stoppage, or, if neither team was moving forward, by the attacking team.

(b) If the player catches a ball direct from a kick by an opponent other than from a kick-off or from a drop out, and is immediately held by an opponent so that a maul ensues and the maul becomes stationary or the ball becomes unplayable his team shall put in the ball at the ensuing scrummage.

Law 23. Touch and Lineout

A. Touch

(1) The ball is in touch:

* when it is not being carried by a player and it touches a touchline or the ground or a person or object on or beyond it; or

* when it is carried by a player and it or the player carrying it touches the touchline or the ground beyond it.

(2) If the ball is not in touch and has not crossed the plane of the touchline a player who is in touch may kick the ball or propel it with his hand but not hold it.

(3) The ball is deemed to have been kicked directly into touch if, from a kick, it is in touch without having pitched on the playing area or without having touched or been touched by a player or the referee.

B. Lineout

The line-of-touch is an imaginary line in the field of play at right angles to the touchline through the place where the ball is thrown in.

Formation of Lineout

(1) A lineout is formed by at least two players from each team lining up in single lines parallel to the line-of-touch in readiness for the ball to be thrown in between them. The team throwing in the ball shall determine the maximum number of players from either team who so line up. Such players are those 'in the lineout', unless excluded below.

(2) Each team must line up at least half a metre on its side of the line-of-touch, so as to leave a clear space of one metre between the two lines of players.

(3) The lineout stretches from five metres from the touchline from which the ball is being thrown in to a position fifteen metres from that touchline.

(4) Any player of either team who is more than fifteen metres from the touch-line when the lineout begins is not in the lineout.

Throwing in the Ball

(5) When the ball is in touch the place at which it must be thrown in is as follows:

(a) When the ball goes into touch from a penalty kick; or from a kick, including a free kick, awarded within twenty-two metres of the kicker's goal-line, at the place where it touched or crossed the touchline, except as otherwise provided.

(b) When the kicker has received the ball outside his twenty-two metres line and retreated behind that line before kicking, and on all other occasions when the ball is kicked directly into touch, after having been kicked as stated in (a), opposite the place from which the ball was kicked or at the place where it touched or crossed the touchline if that place be nearer to the kicker's goal-line.

(c) When a quick throw-in is taken, from any point along the touchline between where the ball went into touch and the goal-line of the team throwing in the ball.

(d) Otherwise when the ball is in touch, at the place when the ball touched or crossed the touchline.

(6)(a) When kicked into touch from a penalty kick, the ball will be thrown in at the lineout by the team which kicked the ball into touch.

(b) Otherwise the ball is to be thrown by an opponent of the player whom it last touched, or by whom it was carried before being in touch.

(c) In the event of doubt as to which team should throw in the ball, the attacking team should do so.

(d) The player throwing in the ball must not put any part of his foot in the field-of-play.

(7) The ball may be brought back into play at a formed lineout or by a quick throw-in which can only be taken before the lineout has formed.

If a quick throw-in occurs after the

lineout is formed it is void and the ball is brought into play at the formed lineout by the same team.

(8) At a formed lineout the ball must be thrown in at the place indicated in (5) so that it first touches the ground or touches or is touched by a player at least five metres from the touchline along the line-of-touch; otherwise the opposing team shall have the right, at its option, to throw in the ball or to take a scrummage.

(9)(a) At a quick throw-in, the ball that went into touch must be used and, after going into touch, it must have been touched only by the player throwing it in; otherwise the ball shall be thrown in at the place indicated in (5) by the same team.

(b) At a quick throw-in the throw must be straight along the line-of-touch at a distance of not less than five metres from the touchline; otherwise the opposition shall have the right, at its option, to throw in the ball or to take a scrummage at the place where the quick throw-in occurred.

(10) If, on the second occasion, the ball is not thrown correctly, a scrummage shall be formed and the ball shall be put in by the team which threw it in on the first occasion.

Beginning and End of Lineout

(11) The lineout begins when the ball leaves the hands of the player throwing it in.

(12) The lineout ends when:
* a ruck or maul is taking place and all the feet of the players in the ruck or maul have moved beyond the line-of-touch; or
* a player carrying the ball leaves the lineout; or
* the ball has been passed back, knocked back or kicked from the lineout; or
* the ball is thrown beyond a position fifteen metres from the touchline; or
* the ball has become unplayable.

Peeling Off

'Peeling off' occurs when a player (or players) moves from his position in the lineout for the purpose of catching the ball when it has been passed or knocked back by another of his team in the line-out.

(13) When the ball is in touch players who approach the line-of-touch must *always* be presumed to do so for the purpose of forming a lineout. Except in a peeling-off movement, such players must not leave the line-of-touch, or the line-out when formed, until the lineout has ended. A player must not begin to peel off until the ball has left the hands of the player throwing it in.

Exception: At a quick throw-in, when a player may come to the line-of-touch and retire from the position without penalty.

(14) In a peeling-off movement a player must move parallel and close to the lineout.

Restrictions on Players in the Lineout

(15) *Before* the ball has been thrown in and has touched the ground or has touched or been touched by a player, any player in the lineout must not:

(a) be off-side; or

(b) use an opponent as a support to enable him to jump for the ball or push, charge, shoulder or obstruct an opponent; or

(c) use any player of his team as a support to enable him to jump for the ball or lift any player of his team or bind with any player of his team; or

(d) stand within five metres of the touch-line to prevent the ball from being thrown five metres.

(16) When jumping for the ball a player must use both hands or his inside arm to catch or deflect the ball.

(17) *After* the ball has touched the ground or touched or been touched by a player, any player at the lineout must not:

(a) be off-side; or

(b) hold, push, shoulder or obstruct an opponent not holding the ball; or

(c) charge an opponent except in an attempt to tackle him or to play the ball.

(18) Except when jumping for the ball or peeling off, a clear space of one metre must be left between the two lines of players until the ball has touched or been touched by a player or has touched the ground.

(19) A player in the lineout may move into the space between the touchline and the five-metres mark only when the ball has been thrown beyond him and, if he does so, he must not move towards his goal-line before the lineout ends, except in a peeling-off movement.

(20) Until the lineout ends, no player may move beyond a position fifteen metres from the touchline except as allowed when the ball is thrown beyond that position in accordance with the Exception following law 24D (1) (c).

(21) A player participating in the lineout as defined in Law 24D may run into the gap in the lineout and take the ball provided he does not charge or obstruct an opponent in the lineout.

Restrictions on Players not in Lineout

(22) Players of either team who are not in the lineout may not advance from behind the lineout and take the ball from a throw-in, except only a player advancing at a long throw-in.

Place of scrummage: Any scrummage taken or ordered under this law or as a result of any infringement in a lineout shall be formed fifteen metres from the touchline along the line-of-touch.

Law 24. Off-side

Off-side means that a player is in a position in which he is out of the game and is liable to penalty.

In general play the player is in an off-side position because he is in front of the ball when it has been last played by another player of his team.

In play at scrummage, ruck, maul or lineout the player is off-side because he remains or advances in front of the line or place started in, and otherwise infringes the relevant sections of this Law.

A. Off-side in General Play

(1) A player is in an off-side position if the ball has been:

* kicked; or
* touched; or
* is being carried by one of his team behind him.

(2) There is no penalty for being in an off-side position unless:

(a) the player plays the ball or obstructs an opponent

(b) he being within ten metres of an opponent waiting to play the ball or of the place where the ball pitches does not retire without delay and without interfering with the opponent; or

(c) he, on all other occasions, moves towards the opponents waiting to play the ball or to the place where the ball pitches, before he is put on-side.

Exceptions:

(i) When an off-side player cannot avoid being touched by the ball or by a player carrying it, he is 'accidentally' off-side. Play should be allowed to continue unless the infringing team obtains an advantage, in which case a scrummage should be formed at that place.

(ii) A player who receives an unintentional throw-in forward is not off-side.

B. Off-side at Scrummage

The term 'off-side line' means a line parallel to the goal-line through the hindmost foot of the player's team in the scrummage.

While a scrummage is forming or taking place:

(1) A player is off-side if:

(a) he joins it from an opponent's side; or

(b) he not being in the scrummage nor the player of either team who puts the ball into the scrummage:

* fails to retire behind the off-side line or to his goal-line whichever is nearer; or
* places either foot in front of the off-side line while the ball is still in the scrummage.

A player may leave a scrummage provided he retires immediately behind the off-side line. If he wishes to rejoin the scrummage, he may do so behind the ball. He may not play the ball as it emerges between the feet of his front-row if he is in front of the off-side line.

Exceptions:

The restrictions on leaving the scrummage in front of the off-side line do not apply to the player taking part in 'wheeling'.a scrummage, providing he immediately plays the ball.

(2) A player is off-side if he, being the player of either side who puts the ball into the scrummage, remains or places either foot in front of the ball while it is in the scrummage.

(3) A player is off-side if he, being the immediate opponent of the player putting in the ball, takes up a position on or moves to the opposite side of the scrummage in front of the off-side line.

C. Off-side at Ruck and Maul

The term 'off-side line' means a line parallel to the goal-lines through the hindmost foot of the player's team in the ruck or maul.

Ruck or Maul otherwise than at Lineout

(1) While a ruck or maul is taking place (including a ruck or maul which continues after a lineout has ended) a player is off-side if he:

(a) joins it from his opponent's side; or

(b) joins in front of the hindmost player of his team; or

(c) does not join the ruck or maul but fails to retire behind the off-side line *without delay*; or

(d) unbinds from the ruck or leaves the maul and does not *immediately* retire behind the off-side line; or, once he is

on-side, if he rejoins the ruck or maul in front of the hindmost player of his team; or

(e) advances beyond the off-side line with either foot and does not rejoin the ruck or maul.

Ruck or Maul at Lineout

(2)The term 'participating in the lineout' has the same meaning as in Section D of this Law. A player participating in the lineout is not obliged to join or remain in the ruck or maul and if he is not in the ruck or maul he continues to participate in the lineout until it has ended. While a lineout is in progress and a ruck or maul takes place, a player is off-side if he:

(a) joins the ruck or maul from his opponent's side; or

(b) joins in front of the hindmost player of his team; or

(c) being a player who is participating in a lineout and is not in the ruck or maul, does not retire to and remain at the off-side line as defined in this section; or

(d) being a player who is not participating in the lineout, remains or advances with either foot in front of the off-side line defined in Section D of this law.

D. Off-side at Lineout

The term 'participating in a lineout' refers exclusively to the following players:

* those players who are in the lineout;
  or
* the player who throws in the ball;
  and
* his immediate opponent who may
  have the option of throwing in the
  ball; or
* one other player of either team who
  takes up a position to receive the ball
  if it is passed or knocked back from
  the lineout.

All other players are not participating in
the lineout.

The term 'off-side line' means a line
ten metres behind the line-of-touch and
parallel to the goal lines or, if the goal-line
be nearer than ten metres to the line-of-
touch, the 'off-side line' is the goal line.

Off-side while participating in Lineout
(1) The participating player is off-side if:
(a) *before* the ball has touched a player or
    the ground he wilfully remains or
    advances with either foot in front of
    the line-of-touch, unless he advances
    while jumping for the ball provided
    that the jump is made from his side of
    the line-of-touch; or
(b) *after* the ball has touched a player or
    the ground, if he is not carrying the
    ball, he advances in front of the ball,
    unless he is lawfully tackling or
    attempting to tackle an opponent
    who is participating in the lineout.

Such tackle or attempt to tackle must,
however, start from his side of the
ball; or
(c) before the lineout ends he moves
    beyond a position fifteen metres from
    the touchline.
Exception:
Players of the team throwing in the ball
may move beyond a position of fifteen
metres from the touchline for a long
throw to them. They may do so only
when the ball leaves the hand of the
player throwing it in and if they do so
their opponents participating in the lineout may follow them. If players so move
and the ball is not thrown to or beyond
them they must be penalised for off-side.
(2) The player throwing in the ball and
his immediate opponent must:
(a) remain within five metres of the
    touchline; or
(b) retire to the off-side line; or
(c) join the lineout after the ball has been
    thrown in five metres; or
(d) move into position to receive the ball
    if it is passed or knocked back from
    the lineout providing no other player
    is occupying that position at the line-
    out.

**Off-side while not participating in
Lineout**
(3) A player who is not participating is
off-side if before the lineout has ended
he advances or remains with either

foot in front of the off-side line.

Exception:

Players of the team throwing in the ball who are not participants in the lineout may advance for a long-throw-in to them beyond the lineout. They may do so only when the ball leaves the hand of the player throwing in the ball and, if they do so, their opponents may advance to meet them. If players so advance for a long throw-in to them and the ball is not thrown to them then they must be penalised for off-side.

Players returning to 'On-Side' Position

(4) A player is not obliged, before throwing in the ball, to wait until players of his team have returned to or behind the lineout but such players are off-side unless they return to an on-side position without delay.

Law 25. On-side

On-side means that a player is in the Game and not liable to penalty for off-side.

Player made on-side by action of his team

(1) Any player who is off-side in general play becomes on-side as a result of any of the following actions of his team:

* when the off-side player has retired behind the player of his team who last kicked, touched or carried the ball; or

* when one of his team carrying the ball has run in front of him; or

* when one of his team has run in front of him when coming from the place or from behind the place where the ball was kicked.

In order to put the off-side player on-side, this other player must be in the playing area. But he is not debarred from following up in touch or touch-in-goal.

Player made on-side by action of opposing team

(2) Any player who is off-side in general play, *except* an off-side player within ten metres of an opponent waiting to play the ball or where the ball pitches, becomes on-side as a result of any of the following actions:

* when an opponent carrying the ball has run five metres; or

* when an opponent kicks or passes the ball; or

* when an opponent *intentionally* touches the ball and does not catch or gather it.

An off-side player within ten metres of an opponent waiting to play the ball or where the ball pitches, *cannot* be put on-side by any action of his opponents. Any *other* off-side player in general play is *always* put on-side when an opponent plays the ball.

Player retiring at Scrummages, Ruck, Maul or Lineout

(3) A player who is in an off-side position when a scrummage, ruck, maul or line-out is forming or taking place and is retiring as required by Law 24 (Off-side) becomes on-side:

* when an opponent carrying the ball has run five metres; or

* when an opponent has kicked the ball.

An off-side player in this situation is not put on-side when an opponent passes the ball.

Law 26. Foul Play

Foul Play is any action by a player which is contrary to the letter and spirit of the Game and includes obstruction, unfair play, misconduct, dangerous play, unsporting behaviour, retaliation and repeated infringements.

Obstruction

(1) It is illegal for any player:

(a) who is running for the ball to charge or push an opponent running for the ball, except shoulder to shoulder;

(b) who is in an off-side position wilfully to run or stand in front of another player of his team who is carrying the ball, thereby preventing an opponent from reaching the latter player;

(c) who is carrying the ball after it has come out of the scrummage, ruck, maul or lineout to attempt to force his way through the players of his team in front of him;

(d) who is an outside player in a scrummage or ruck to prevent an opponent from advancing round the scrummage or ruck.

Unfair Play, Repeated Infringements

(2) It is illegal for any player:

(a) deliberately to play unfairly or wilfully infringe any Law of the Game

(b) wilfully to waste time

(c) wilfully to knock or throw the ball from the playing area into touch, touch-in-goal or over the dead-ball line

(d) to infringe repeatedly any Law of the Game.

Misconduct , Dangerous Play

(3) It is illegal for any player:

(a) to strike an opponent

(b) wilfully to hack or kick an opponent or trip him with the foot, or to trample on an opponent lying on the ground

(c) to tackle early, late or dangerously, including the action known as a 'stiff-arm tackle'

(d) who is not running for the ball wilfully to charge or obstruct an opponent who has just kicked the ball

(e) to hold, push, charge, obstruct or grasp an opponent not holding the ball, except in a scrummage, ruck or maul (Except in a scrummage or ruck the dragging away of a player lying close to the ball is permitted. Otherwise pulling any part of the clothing of an opponent is holding.)

(f) in the front-row of a scrummage to form down some distance from the opponents and rush against them

(g) in the front-row of a scrummage wilfully to lift an opponent off his feet or force him upwards out of the scrummage

(h) wilfully to cause a scrummage, ruck or maul to collapse

(i) while the ball is out of play to molest, obstruct or in any way interfere with an opponent or be guilty of any form of misconduct

(j) to commit misconduct on the playing area which is prejudicial to the spirit of good sportsmanship.

Player Ordered Off

A player who is ordered off shall take no further part in the match. When a player is ordered off, the referee shall, as soon as possible after the match, send to the Union or other disciplinary body having jurisdiction over the match a report naming the player and describing the circumstances which necessitated the ordering off. The Union or other discipli-nary body having jurisdiction over the match shall consider such report and any action and impose such punishment as they see fit.

Citing of Players

Where a player has committed an act of foul play which has not been detected by match officials, either of the Unions or affiliated organisations participating in the match have the discretion to cite that player to show cause why he should not be held accountable in the same way as a player who has been ordered off.

Law 27. Penalty Kick

A penalty kick is awarded to the non-offending team as stated in the Laws. It may be taken by any player of the non-offending team provided that the kicker, if holding the ball, must propel it out of his hands or, if the ball is on the ground, he must propel it a visible distance from the mark. He may keep his hands on the ball while kicking it.

(1) The non-offending team has the option of taking a scrummage at the mark and shall put in the ball.

(2) When a penalty kick is taken the following shall apply:

(a) The kick must be taken without undue delay.

(b) The kick must be taken at or behind the mark on a line through the mark and the kicker may place the ball for a place-kick. If the place prescribed by the law for the award of the penalty kick is within five metres of the opponents' goal line, the mark for the penalty kick or scrummage taken instead of it shall be five metres from the goal-line on a line with that place.

(c) A kicker may kick the ball in any direction and he may play the ball again, without any restriction, except that if he has indicated to the referee that he intends to attempt a kick at goal or has taken the action indicating that intention he must not kick the ball in any other way. A player kicking for touch may only punt or drop kick the ball. Any indication of intention is irrevocable.

(d) The *kicker's team*, except the placer for the place kick, must be behind the ball until it has been kicked. Retiring players of the kicker's team who are in front of the ball will not be penalised if their failure to retire is due to the rapidity with which the kick has been taken but they must not stop retiring and enter the game until:

* the off-side player has retired behind the player who kicked the ball; or
* one of his team carrying the ball has run in front of him; or
* one of his team has run in front of him after coming from behind the place where the ball was kicked.

(e) The *opposing team* must run without delay (and continue to do so while the kick is being taken and while the ball is being played by the kicker's

team) to or behind the line parallel to the goal-lines and ten metres from the mark, or to their own goal if nearer to the mark. If a kick at goal is taken they must there remain motionless with their hands by their sides until the kick has been taken. Retiring players will not be penalised if their failure to retire ten metres is due to the rapidity with which the kick is taken, but they must not stop retiring and re-enter the game until an opponent carrying the ball has run five metres.

(f) The *opposing team* must not prevent the kick or interfere with the kicker in any way. This applies to actions such as wilfully carrying, throwing or kicking the ball away out of reach of the kicker.

Law 28. Free Kick

A free kick is a kick awarded for a fair-catch or to a non-offending team as stated in the Laws. A goal may not be scored from a free kick.

The team awarded the free kick may not score a dropped goal until after the ball next becomes dead or the ball has been played or touched by an opposing player. This restriction applies similarly following a scrummage taken in lieu of a free kick.

A free kick awarded for an infringement may be taken by any player of the non-offending team. A free kick may be taken by any form of kick, unless kicking for touch, provided that the kicker, if holding the ball, must propel it out of his hands or, if the ball is on the ground, he must propel it a visible distance from the mark. He may keep his hand on the ball while kicking it.

(1) The team awarded the free kick has the option of taking a scrummage at the mark and shall put in the ball.

(2) When a kick is taken, it must be taken without undue delay.

(3) The kick must be taken at or behind the mark on a line through the mark and the kicker may place the ball for a place kick.

(4) If the place prescribed by the Laws for the award of a free kick is within five metres of the opponents' goal-line, the mark for the free kick, or the scrummage taken instead of it, shall be five metres from the goal-line on a line through that place.

(5) The kicker may kick the ball in any direction and may play the ball without restriction. A player kicking for touch may only punt or drop kick the ball.

(6) The *kicker's team*, except a placer for a place kick, must be behind the ball until it has been kicked. Retiring players of the kicker's team who are in front of the ball will not be penalised if their failure to retire is due to the rapidity with which

the kick has been taken but they must not stop retiring and enter the game until:

* the off-side player has retired behind the player who kicked the ball; or
* one of his team carrying the ball has run in front of him; or
* one of his team has run in front of him after coming from behind the place where the ball was kicked.

(7) The *opposing team* must not wilfully resort to any action which may delay the taking of a free kick. This includes actions such as wilfully carrying, throwing or kicking the ball away out of reach of the kicker.

(8) The *opposing team* must retire without delay to or behind the line parallel to the goal-lines and ten metres from the mark or to their own goal-line if the mark is In-goal. Having so retired, players of the opposing team may charge, with a view to preventing the kick, as soon as the kicker begins his run or offers to kick. Retiring players will not be penalised if their failure to retire ten metres is due to the rapidity with which the kick is taken, but they may not stop retiring and enter the game until an opponent carrying the ball has run five metres.

(9) If, having charged fairly, players of the opposing team prevent the kick being taken, it is void.

(10) Neither the kicker nor the placer shall wilfully do anything which may lead the opposing team to charge prema-

turely. If either does so, the charge shall not be disallowed.

___

Amendments, variations, experimental laws and directives from the International Rugby Football Board may be found in the *Laws of the Game*, published annually by the International Rugby Football Board. This invaluable book also contains detailed notes for the guidance of referees and a complete list of rules for Mini Rugby and Midi Rugby. Copies may be obtained from:

Rugby Football Union Shop
South West Concourse
Twickenham
Middlesex TW1 1DZ

Bibliography

Rugby Union: The Skills of the Game, Barrie Corless (The Crowood Press, 1985)

Total Rugby: 15-Man Rugby for Coaches and Players, Jim Greenwood (A & C Black, 1985)

Rugby: The All Blacks Way, J. J. Stewart (The Crowood Press, 1987)

Rugby Tactics, Peter Winder (A & C Black, 1991)

Rugby Union: Play the Game, Ian Morrison (Ward Lock, revised 1993)

The Complete Book of Mini Rugby, Don Rutherford (Partridge Press, 1993)

Rugby Union: Know the Game (A & C Black, 1994)

History

Rugby: A Way of Life, edited by Nigel Starmer-Smith (Stanley Paul, 1986)

Running With the Ball, Jennifer Macrory (Collins, Willow, 1991)

Fitness

Get Ready for Rugby Union: A Complete Training Programme, Stuart Biddle/Barrie Corless/Anne de Looy/Peter Thomas (The Crowood Press, 1989)

General

Rothman's Rugby Union Yearbook (Headline)

Useful Addresses

Australian Rugby Football Union
Rugby Union House
Crane Place
Sydney
New South Wales 27777
Australia

French Rugby Federation
(Fédération Française de Rugby)
7 Cité d'Antin
75009 Paris
France

Irish Rugby Football Union
62 Lansdowne Road
Dublin 4
Republic of Ireland

New Zealand Rugby Football Union
Huddart Parker Building
Post Office Square
PO Box 2172
Wellington
New Zealand

Rugby Football Union
Twickenham
Middlesex TW1 1DZ
England

Scottish Rugby Union
Murrayfield
Edinburgh EH12 5PJ
Scotland

South African Rugby Board
Boundary Road
Newlands 7700
South Africa

Welsh Rugby Union
National Stadium
Cardiff CF1 1JL
Wales

Rosie Golby (Secretary WRU)
Meadow House, Springfield Farm
Shipston-on-Stour
Warwickshire CV36 4HQ

Acknowledgements

Extracts from the official Laws of the Game are reproduced by kind permission of the Rugby Football Board.

Photography
The author and publishers are grateful to the following for permission to reproduce copyright photography:
Allsport: pp.54 (T/L), 58, 65, 67, 102, 116, 130, 138, 141, 158, 164.
Colorsport: pp.55, 57, 59, 63, 71, 80, 84, 89, 93, 100, 108, 113, 118, 123, 126, 146, 149, 167, 171.
Popperfoto: pp.16, 19.
Press Association: p.23
Sporting pictures: pp.28, 53, 54 (T/R), 69, 101, 105.

Illustrations
By Raymond Turvey.

Graphic Design
Design/Section, Frome.

Index